ANCHOR BOOKS

THE CRACKED MIRROR

First published in Great Britain in 1994 by
ANCHOR BOOKS
1-2 Wainman Road, Woodston,
Peterborough, PE2 7BU

All Rights Reserved

Copyright Contributors 1994

Foreword

Anchor Books is a small press, established in 1992, with the aim of promoting readable poetry to as wide an audience as possible.

We hope to establish an outlet for writers of poetry who may have struggled to see their work in print.

Following our request in the National Press, we were overwhelmed by the response. The poems presented here have been selected from many entries. Editing proved to be a difficult and daunting task and as the Editor, the final selection was mine.

The poems chosen represent a cross-section of styles and content. They have been sent from all over the country, written by young and old alike, united in the passion for writing poetry.

I trust this selection will delight and please the authors and all those who enjoy reading poetry.

Michelle Abbott
Editor

Contents

Borderland	Adrian Newton	1
The Love of the Hills	Euphemia Harper	1
Woodland Delight	S M Donovan	2
Meadow Way	Caroline Nelson	2
Autumn Views	Bernice Lord	3
The Exile's Dream of Home	Daisy Cooper	4
The Shortest Day on Fair Isle	Edward Cummins	4
Edinburgh	Margaret Lynch	5
One Fifth of Scotland	Graeme J Mitchell	6
The Chunnel Coming	Phyllis Allen	8
Place Fell, Glenridding	Robert Shooter	9
Foulridge Wharf	Maureen Green	9
Lake District Life	Pauline Sanderson	10
My Journey	Kay E Tallentire	11
Queen of the Garden	Muriel Roberts	12
White Butterflies	Erik Jon Roberts	13
Blowy	S F McDowell	14
Autumn	David C Southall	14
The Ochils	Val Pöhler	15
Success	G S Mutch	16
Woodland Scenes	Edward Lusk	16
Early Morning in Caithness	C Morris	17
Autumn Tapestry	Reneé Loynds	18
Listen in the Morning Light	Barbara Barlow	18
Winter	Elaine Shackleton	19
On and on	Ann Shacklady	19
Estate	Ray Talus	20
These I Have Loved	W P Kneen	21
Lifeboat and Station	Freda Grieve	21
My Mum's Trip to the Palace	Brian Dougan	22

Title	Author	Page
A Holiday of a Lifetime	Hannah Melling	23
Memories of Pendle Hill	Mary Halsall	24
Happenings	Gwen Walsh	25
My Isle	Shelley Walker	26
Big Ben	David Batten	26
Rural Tayside	Donald McKerchar	27
The Meaning of Strathclyde	Maureen Egan	28
The Doctor's Surgery	Iris Grice	29
Race Day	Mark Newberry	30
Looking After the Land	Phyllis Carpenter	31
Untitled	Margaret Dewar	32
The Squirrel	Betty Samson	33
September Fires	Margaret Gilles-Brown	33
Barbados Holiday	Derek Fellows	34
The Hustler	Ray Ashworth	35
Reluctant Traveller	Trish Johnson	35
Breakfast With Ducks on The River Lune - West Bank	Iris Robertson	37
Pride and Prejudice	Ruth Maria Midgley	38
Between the Passes	Gill Pickup	38
Double Dutch	Elizabeth Thorpe	39
Remembrance Day	A C Brennan	40
My Cottage	Marion Talbot	40
Greetings on Meetings	G Rowe	41
River Holiday	Winifred Woolfelden	42
A Song of Surrey	Marge A Chamberlain	43
Gargoyle	Talitha Tallett	44
Sunday Bus	Joe Heeley	45
Solace	Dorris Braithwaite	45
Untitled	M McKenna	46
Morecambe Bay - Flookburgh Fishermen	Freda Bunce	47
Come to Sunny Bowdon	Tony Sheldon	47

On a Pennine Hill	Eric Johnson	48
The Revenant	Dorothy Hilditch	49
The Caterpillar	Rosemary Atherton	49
Animals	Hayley Fairhurst	50
The Four Seasons	Debbie L McGrory	50
Summer Solstice	Zoë Turpin	52
What a Wonderful Thing a Flower	J Dormer	52
Seasons	Melda Larsen	53
Autumn	Catherine Butterworth	54
Autumn	Rose Hoskins	54
Untitled	Millicent Sinclair	55
The Star	Lily Alyward	56
Leaves	Rodger Moir	56
Lakeland Speaks	Elizabeth Monoghan	57
Eventide	J R Arrowsmith	58
Snowing	Alexander Southgate	58
The Harvest Moon	Brian Watson	59
My Tree	Jennie Doran	60
The Field	Annie Harrison	60
End of Another Year	A Woodcock	61
Autunm	Georgina Gorton	61
The Robin	G E Cannell	62
Contrasts	Anthony Smith	62
Nature and Spring	Eileen D Shaw	63
Ideal Home	Frances Fothergill	64
Our Street	Glenda Boardman	65
Al Tuwallil Qatar	B S Burton	65
Lancashire North West	John R Calvert	66
Rutland Water	Elizabeth Kent	67
Our Great Britain	Edward Dixon (Melly)	67
Preston 1950	William E Moore	68
Beach at Theologos	John A Stevenson	69
Brechin City	Agnes Peal	70
Banff	Allie Bartlett	70
My Town	M A Aldridge	71

Title	Author	Page
For the Bliss of Loneliness	Harry Crompton Fils	71
To the Owl	Winnie Lee	71
My Cat Dances	Andrew Callen	72
Autumn	Ruby L Robinson	73
Lancashire	A Baker	73
My Pendle Hill	B Graham	74
Untitled	P Tipping	75
Chimneys	D Bertwistle	75
A Visit to Lancashire	Barbara C Boon	77
Nature's Picture	Maud Eleanor Hobbs	78
Fox Hunt	Jane McDowell	78
My Secret Garden	Liza Leece	79
School	J Chapman	80
The Mersey	John F Perkins	80
For Dornie	Guyan John Porter	81
Deep in the Heart of Govan	Ruby A Graham	82
Tartan's Rising	Glen Summers	82
Loch Leven	Alexander K Sampson	83
The Restless World	Edna Dixon	84
Reflections of Promise	Simon Bull	85
The Silvery Tay	J Emslie Lamond	86
My Hame Toon	Joan Christie	87
Ormiston	Thomas Davidson	88
Dingwall Slumbers	Rosaline H MaddDonald	89
A Walk Down Scotsburn Glen	Brian Kershaw	90
My Village Home	Dorothy Keith	90
Discord	Joy Carruthers	91
Riches	Steven Dawson	92
Lament for Lost Trees	M Sharpe	92
Aberdeen	George Cooney	93
Renfrewshire	Eileen Mulholland	94
Garden in Bloom	Vera Skelton	95
Summer's Day	Irene Attwell	96
The Picture Window	D Highman	97

Mannanin's Sky	Amanda Cornish	97
This Place is Mine	Christopher Newman	98
Ode to Craigievar Castle by a National Trust Guide	Lorna Alexander	98
Cathedral	Lillian Coombs	99
Dumfrieshire	Jane S Simpson	100
East Kilbride	Jacqueline Gill	100
Stevenston	Rayma Barclay	101
East Lothian	J McWithers	102
Banished Waters	M M Williams	102
November	Margaret R Williams	103
My Imaginary Animal	Helené Duerden	104
Keeping Time	Pat MacKenzie	104
The County of Fife	Ian MacFarlane	105
Border River	Janet Murray	106
The Waiting Room	Linda M T Edwards	107
Love	B Lancashire Frain	108
Snowflakes	Margaret Joy	108
The Eagle's Cry	Matthew Henderson	109
Life	Margaret Walker	110
The Great Rift Valley	Tom Powell	110
Observation Tower	Jenni Meredith	111
Rules	Eileen Kyte	112
Somerset	Dorothy Blackwell	112
Wanderer's Dream	Morwenna Bateson	113
Cottage Life	Tresca Tucker	114
Countryside Desecration	David L Rae	115
The Sea	Leo Roberts	116

Borderland
The river whispers
Of distant oceans
A salmon leaps.

The wind is rising
On open moorland
A curlew cries.

The mist still lingers
In distant forest
A leaf falls.

Tall stones recall
The ghosts of hunters
A lark is singing.

The clouds are lifting
As twilight deepens
I turn for home.
Adrian Newton

The Love of the Hills
I treasure the hills of the Borders,
The smooth rolling hills of green.
But I love more the crags of the Highlands,
Where eagle and buzzard are seen.

Stac Pollaidh so stark and so striking,
With battlement ridges on top,
Whale-back Wyvis, and sugar-loaf Suilven,
And Ben Nevis to crown the lot.

The hills are too many to number,
And all have their special appeal.
But I love them so, be they high or low,
Jagged nerves they soothe and heal.

They are pleasant to climb in summer,
A challenge in winter's snow.
But whatever the season,
Take care and reason,
They can be both friend and foe.
Euphemia Harper

Woodland Delight
The sun is up and shining through
It brings a sparkle to the dew,
Spiders' webs are glistening bright
To watch them it is sheer delight.
Two blackbirds fluttering here and there
I am sure they will make a perfect pair
It's nice to stand and feel the breeze
As birds are nesting in the trees.
The primroses and bluebells are peeping through
Soon there will be a carpet of perfect blue
White snowdrops are daintily drooping their head
So do be careful where you tread.
Little animals scampering here and there
Hoping to find a mate to share
Oh what a lovely sight to see
Green shoots sprouting on every tree,
I pick a snowdrop for its fragrant smell
Sadly have to say farewell.
S M Donovan

Meadow Way
The meadows where we used to play
There are neat little patios there today,
But shining concrete after April showers
Can never replace those sweet spring flowers.

We picked up gold and silver beneath our feet
At the pond the purple iris was protected
We knew the water was too deep,
Man made bricks and mortar constructed to a design
Compared to green pastures could never be sublime.
Caroline Nelson

Autumn Views
A ray of sunshine, an early dawn
Chill wind caressing on luscious green lawn
Fronded with dewdrops jewels in the night
Tree branches swaying in September plight,
Autumn leaves falling, swirling, revolving
Variegated colours together evolving
Dancing ballerinas on tip of toe
An emblem of foliage against unseen foe;
Rich golden browns, burnt orange and creams
Tainted yellows and reds curled over greens
Mottled and aged through long summer sun.

Down from the trees on which they were borne
Featherlike fashion from where they were shorn
Drifting silently to soft ground enticing
Now and again their colours colliding,
Twisting and turning to fall to God's earth
Like hundreds of dancers for all they are worth
Changing direction by wind they are blown
Far from the branches from which they have flown,
Formation altering in synchronisation
Next lying and resting in great exultation
Gone are the days now of last summer's sun.
Bernice Lord

The Exile's Dream of Home
Oh to see my homeland
Out there some place north-west
Oh to live and die
With folks I love the best,
Oh to tramp the hills and dales
Where I could dream and wait
To hear once more the hoot of owl
Calling to his mate.
Oh to see the distant crags
Before it is too late
And sleep again beneath the stars
My dream would be complete.
Oh to wander further still
To reach the highest peaks
My long and lonely years
Would barely seem like weeks,
But I'm far away from my homeland
Where birds are free to nest
In one of God's rare corners
It's where my soul would rest.
Daisy Cooper

The Shortest Day on Fair Isle
The blandest arc of sun shone overhead,
the shortest of our days obeyed the clock.
Sheep gathered on the shingles, sniffed and fed
from off the fresh entanglements of wrack.

The windmill slotted shadows through the air.
They fell amongst the melting of the snow.
The cutting of the blades intoned a prayer
as secrets in the earth began to stir.

Our vessel in the haven tugged at ropes.
She rolled and lolled, a puppet in the swell.
The cargo swung aloft in giant grabs . . .
the sun's return was all we dared foretell.

'The crane has blown a bearing,' someone said.
The forklift's thrown a fanbelt in the hold.
Beneath dark silhouettes the light has fled.
A loom of ice from Skadan flashes cold.

The wind has played its game with us all day.
We lent towards it as we walked ashore.
They tell us it will veer away and die.
The sheep lie huddled, somewhere over there.

We manufacture artificial light.
A generator chisels at the dark.
The oil-lamp of our ancestors was bright
enough to close their day. But we must work.

The rain is falling now. The stars are blind.
Our ropes are doubled-up against the tide.
Huge rubber fenders flatten as they grind
the seed of hibernation's mouldy bread.
Edward Cummins

Edinburgh
I live in a beautiful city
the scenery is divine
and as I was born and bred here
I think of it always as *mine*.

The seaside, the hills and the lochs are nearby
The castle stands proud on its rock,
Princes Street Gardens are laid out below
and the wonderful floral clock.

Pentland hills, Swanston village and Cramond
and Silverknowes walk by the sea,
Queensferry with both the Forth bridges
there's no better place you could be.

The people are kind and they're friendly
there's plenty to see and to do,
and this capital city of Scotland
is ready to welcome you.

The old town is brimful of history
with the Castle, Royal Mile and the shops
the new town is known for its grand architecture
no wonder that Edinburgh is tops.
Margaret Lynch

One Fifth of Scotland
Fae the Mull O' Kintyre,
right oot tae Harthill
a journey of excellence,
a really great thrill
across lochs an' o'er mountains,
tae Oban we'd go
an' away doon past Girvan,
through the Ayrshire we know.

Ye can almost see Tam,
gallop his mare o'er the brig
as the witches an' warlocks
dance their wee jig.
There was even Dr Lister,
in the Glasgow of old
an' the monorail in Milngavie,
left oot in the cold.

There's Paisley wae its Abbey,
an' Erskine wae its Brig
an' John Brown's old shipyard
now makin' an oil rig.
We've got the collection of Burrell,
in the Pollock Estate
an' coal mines galore,
though they're closing of late.

The Clyde winding its way,
like a lace through a shoe
stretching through the region,
through the old an' the new.
Surrounded by mountains,
and hills all around
run rivers an' lochs,
through wonderful ground.

But we also run buses,
an' trains here as well
an' schools by the hundreds,
too many tae tell.
An' a muckle great police force,
and fire brigade too
but alas Scottish ambulances,
are too bloody few.

Art galleries, an' museums,
an' churches by the score,
distilleries, an' breweries,
and much, much more.
Universities fur the scholars,
and dole queues fur the boys
both shuffled around
like Conservative toys.

But it's Labour that's in power,
in this neck of the woods
an' it really does nae matter,
'cause nane deliver the goods.
Then there's Rangers an' Celtic,
an' Clydebank too,
Morton an' Killie,
tae mention but a few.

So what is this place,
this region called Strathclyde
it's about one fifth of Scotland,
it's where good folk abide.

Graeme J Mitchell

The Chunnel Coming

Tall, towering, trembling trees,
Whispering, murmuring, swayed by the breeze.
Proudly they stood there admired by all,
None of us knew that the axe would soon fall!
Make way for the Chunnel, churn up the mud,
The trees hit the ground with a dull, sullen thud.
People protested, wrote to MP's
Held angry meetings - none heeded their pleas!
'There's work for the lads, good money too,
To be gained from the workers as they burrow through.
They'll need their victuals, their beer and their fun,
As they dig out the hole where the fast trains will run.'
Down went the concrete, the railway, the roads,
Ponds were filled in with no thought for the toads.
Wild flowers vanished along with the streams
Bulldozed and burned with young people's dreams.
The hills around Folkestone became quite a mess.
Financiers said, "Twill be a success,
In the long-term, there will be a gain,'
But projects like this do not come without pain.
Some of the workers were killed in the hole
On the job that they took to keep off the dole.
The tunnel is finished, we wait for the day,
The *Official Opening,* sometime in May.
Blue harebells and butterflies exchanged for the train
That will cross the Channel and come back again.
Garden of England, that's what they called Kent.
Next century, people will ask what that meant?

Phyllis Allen

Place Fell, Glenridding
Woman, you watch the fells lie back, like you
basking at ease during sunny rest - stop;
walkers have tramped your breasts just for the view
of dawn's soft breaking over mountain top.
You watch a ewe so gently give lamb birth
on sheltered slopes where children hide and play,
where lovers come to worship mother earth,
imbibe her joys, her peaks, her rhythmic sway.
The aged couple slowly climb Place Fell
to find, once more, lost truth, before their call,
to breathe fresh air, see spring flowers, in this dell,
seek nature's arms' protection till their fall.
Place Fell you hold eternally pure air
or would if man and woman really care.
Robert Shooter

Foulridge Wharf
On Foulridge Wharf
    I take my walk,
Thank you Lord, I can see,
    Beauty that surrounds me.

Grasses so green,
    Would enhance my dream,
Gently swaying in the breeze,
    Whispering to the trees.

The canal rippling by,
    Reflecting from the sky,
Wonders of nature,
    In all its majesty.

Ducklings gather round,
    Now I have found,
A welcome to my outstretched hand,
    As they waddle onto land.

I wonder if they understand,
    Bells that ring,
And people sing,
    Not far away.

Changing of the seasons,
    Will give me reasons,
To stop and stare,
    And make me care.

Foulridge the village,
    I do love,
Bad memories of the past
    I hope will not last.

I leave the green grasses swaying,
    To church to do my praying,
For peace without pain,
    To prevail once again.
Maureen Green

Lake District Life

Us northerners are tough as boots
It goes back to our earthy roots.
Midst hills and valleys, lakes galore,
It never rains here, it just pours.

We're outdoor people, through and through,
And walking's what we like to do.
We don't sit in watching tellies,
We're out there in coats and wellies.

We're always walking in the rain,
O'er hills and vales and tough terrain.
Never daunted by any task,
Never without a thermos flask.

We drink a vast amount of tea,
Refills are needed constantly.
Well, when you live in these cold climes,
You have to combat it sometimes.

Hardy, they call us and it's true,
We're very good at making do.
Living out here in the sticks,
We're all just simple, country hicks.

Midst rain and hail and wind and snow,
No wonder that our noses glow.
Our motto is: 'We will endure,'
Even if we're knee-deep in manure.
Pauline Sanderson

My Journey
The old farmhouse is the only viewpoint
In the ice white landscape, for it is
Dark.
It is a silent bastion shielding its occupants,
As it always has, through countless such storms.

Small, remote, like a charcoal drawing
Against the great white hills
Beyond.
A pine wood makes a dark
Smudge, but the rest is without feature.

A gust of wind stirs the snow
Into a cloud of fine mist. I am
Alone.
The farm, the moor, the hills beyond,
Have all disappeared.

I walk on, falling often.
The soft flakes of snow drop
Silently.
In every sense this is a journey alone
For now I am aware of my fraility.

Journey's end. I have changed perspective,
I look to the snow line beyond. Strength is
Here.
Beckoned inside by the weathered walls, silently
And with relief, I walk to the ancient door.

I am safe, at last, in the charcoal drawing
It has enveloped me in its
Spirit.
I am welcome here
For this is my childhood home.
Kay E Tallentire

Queen of the Garden
Gently unfolding oh sweet butterfly
What magic in your transformation
This morn' you awake, the old life forsake
A wonder of nature's creation.
Sweet creature the heavens have fashioned you well,
And soon in a whirlpool descending
A vision in flight, a burst of delight
Enchanting butterfly.

Weaving and whirling, you know how to tease
Caressing the petals with elegant ease
To taste of the nectar, to bathe in the dew
Nature arrayed all her treasures for you.
Pausing a while, and then it would seem
The moment is shattered, gone like a dream.
Why were you startled? What makes you so shy?
Enchanting butterfly.

On glistening wings, like gossamer gold
Our cares of the world you are stealing
The secrets you hold, forever untold
What mystery your beauty concealing
Oh queen of the garden, I dream of the day
I reach out for you, and you linger.
That fragment of time, will always be mine.
Enchanting butterfly.
Muriel Roberts

White Butterflies
Snow flakes fall from winter skies
Like hovering, swirling butterflies
To land upon the ice bound soil
As though to rest there for a while,
Soon their wings all join together
Covering the heath and heather
Deepening with each flake that falls,
Drifting up stone crofts and walls,
Soon the earth wears winter white
Lighting up the dark of night,
The hedgerows disappear from view
The world seems flat, new born, one hue,
White butterflies silently land
Freeze to earth, melt on the hand,
Thicker yet they still descend,
You fear perhaps they'll never end,
The lea side of the black bare trees,
Shielding sheep crouched on their knees,
Quite suddenly you realise,
Those butterflies are death's disguise.
Erik Jon Roberts

Blowy

bitter winter wind blows by
fills a drab grey January sky
no room for sparrow or gull to fly
only paper and plastic bags sail high

bitter winter wind blows hard
across the garden and through the yard
leading us to be on our guard
or be blown away like a piece of card

bitter winter wind blows through
it blows through me and it blows through you
blows away the old to make way for the new
it blows away the fences and the houses too

bitter winter wind blows free
a bus blows past my window it was a number forty three
followed very closely by a sycamore tree
now I've seen as much as I dare to see.
S F McDowell

Autumn

Soft glow of light reflected from another time in space
in clear night sky of Milky Way and galaxies
upon a journey long in years since birth
when dust to dust first made the first born star.

Tanned golden leaf absorbed of heat by day
denatured, dried and fallen back to earth
from whence it came one early wan sun spring
returned again to clay from whence it grew.

Beside a field of yellow amber ripened wheat
where shelter gave to song thrush and hedge sparrow
and rest to aching back of brown skinned ploughman
paused with cheese and cider at midday.

No lark song now as was in summer gone too soon
the swift and swallow wing to where the sun
beats down on palmed oasis standing in Sahara sand
as darkening evenings warn of winter's wind.

Burn now old man of green your ashes blow across the land
to sleep beneath Jack's frozen crystal gown
of diamond sparkling snow before the new year's herald blows
his welcome in the resurrecting dawn.
David C Southall

The Ochils
April hills are far away,
swimming through the rain
like giant whales.

August hills come nearer
bounding to my side
like eager pups.

November hills are loosely packed
fondant candy, masked
with jaggy beards.

December hills are jumbled cones.
Ice-cream dollops splodged
with chocolate sauce.

Hills are . . . chameleons.
Hills are . . . forever.
I like hills.
Val Pöhler

Success
I came to Central Region in '54
And wondered what the future held in store,
A small workshop was the first thing to get
By good luck I found a small room to let.
Now some customers I had to find
Calling on works was quite a bind
However one large company gave me a break
I knew this was the chance I had to take.
Going from Glasgow to Falkirk each day
Was a strain it was all work and no play
Things improved when I got a house in town
Now was the time to knuckle down,
Business got better and better each day
Central Region was the place to stay
I am writing all this in rhyme
Now that I have some leisure time.
To all my past customers I sincerely thank
For building up my overdraft at the bank
My Betty and I appreciate all you have done
Thank you very much and forgive the pun,
The name of the firm is still going on
And will still be there when I've gone
Central Region is the place to enjoy the good life
So come along bring the family don't forget the wife.
G S Mutch

Woodland Scenes
Listen! Can you hear the wind soft and -
gentle, caressing each leafy branch.
It talks through the boughs in differing -
tones. The trodden twigs reply, in
staccato compliments.
The instrument of walking feet.

Greens of every shade greet our eyes.
Mellowing bark too, 'Here! We Cry.'
Past years they have known, covered lovingly
in mosses of quilt.
They have their share in nature's scheme.

Was that a squirrel in yonder tree.
My little favourite inquisitor.
Such grace and elegance I wish I had.
But I am not a squirrel.
Careful feet; avoid the hedgehog, comical
concealment under his spines.
But a gentle soul for all that.

O come away to Woodland scenes,
You'll find peace there under the greens.
The paths well trodden over the years.
Have filled hearts with joy, maybe tears.
For the old and the young, will walk
In the sun, and rejoice in those
Woodland scenes.
Edward Lusk

Early Morning in Caithness
Daylight is breaking over the bay
No human sound can I hear
Seagulls are waking to a new summer's day
The sun's rays soon will appear.

I love this time of the morning
Before most people awake
Is that smoke coming out of that chimney
Or a wisp of mist from the lake.

The air is like wine here in Caithness
Pollution seems so far away
It's six o'clock in the morning
As we prepare to start a new day.

The sun pulls the curtains of night from the sky
The new day has really begun
Work calls as I see a car passing by
I'm afraid that I'd better run.
C Morris

Autumn Tapestry
You blaze a trail through woodland dell
of crimson fire and burnished gold.
Your starched leaves crackle where they fell
with copper conkers, acorn shells.

Your picture mystic through the haze
of flaming sun and hoary frost.
The squirrels scamper in a maze
of nuts and seeds for winter days.

Woodsmoke scenting the evening air.
Spiralling sparks explode in space.
Hot potatoes carried with care
Guy burnt out, no one sheds a tear.

Tapestry's hues sullied and dull,
wet mulch is formed from crackling leaves.
Inside all autumn's fruit to hull
apples and spice begin to mull.
Incense of autumn ascends through the eaves.
Reneé Loynds

Listen in the Morning Light
Mute hangs the night, the solemn eye of moon surveys the land,
And lights upon the dreary sights of man's destructive hand.
For, far and wide, his greedy tide, has cleaved the beauteous scene,
And woods and meadows lie shorn stark, bereft of blessed green.

Brown larks that rose to greet the dawn have fled to other haunts,
Even the sweet-toned nightingale has gone beneath man's taunts.
No owl now hoots from sombre wood, no fox barks in the glen.
The badgers and the otters are gone from hunting men.
And marshalled all the buildings stand beneath the moon's 'lone eye,
Oh, listen to the west wind, and hear the sobbing sigh.
Oh, listen in the morning light and hear the dying call,
Of nature in the wilderness of man, who made it all.
Barbara Barlow

Winter
Short of daylight hours
Long darkness, waiting.
The colours of grey, white
of ice and snow
Falling
through the blue,
Cool, crystal, clear air.
Elaine Shackleton

On and on
I went walking round the falls one lovely sunny day
The sun shone through the autumn leaves and took my breath away,
The river bounded onward forever down its track
I really think its endless there is no turning back.
On and on it travels as it's done since days gone by,
On and on forever beneath the changing sky
No matter what the seasons the water carries on
On and on forever its job is never done.
Ann Shacklady

Estate
Old house, I've shared your secrets, some
As you have mine
We counted out life's time together, too
Each season soon, a tale became, a fleeting sigh
Of one more chapter, merging old with new
And things confided to your walls, safe kept
Have joined with other joys and sorrows wept.

Old friend, I've heard your timbers yawn
Your spirits sigh,
The winds hurled at your frame, as with my own
Seen fire in the breast, hot coals to embers die
Once shared emotions fading, now alone
But letters in your ashes still remain
Within my mind, to tease my soul again.

Dear home, you spread your arms to me
And those I knew
And strangers, all, found welcome at your hearth
God's creatures nourished here found love, and peace and few
Forgot your shady, friendly, tree lined path
But now I have much time to contemplate
And seldom hear the creaking of the gate.

True shield, you countered life's foul spite
For me and mine
With shutters drawn, we could deny the world
Or else, with windows wide flung let our wills define
New roads to tread with friends, new flags unfurled
'Tis best I take my leave now while I please
Yet savouring the sweeter all of these.
Ray Talus

These I Have Loved
The rough hewn bark of Scottish pine,
Smooth skinned bark of downland beech,
The burred trunk of ancient elm,
The wrinkles 'round your eyes;
These I have loved.

The blackbirds' song in spring,
Warning rivals off his domain each morn',
Cry of curlew at descending dusk,
The ebb and flow of waves on gravel beach;
Your teasing laugh, your voice;
These I have loved.

Pine woods on a hot summer's day,
Wood smoke on a cold winter's night
Roses, lavender, eucalyptus, thyme,
The fragrance of sun-dried meadow hay,
The smell of sweat on skin and hair;
These I have loved.

The purple of the ling upon the moors,
Soft green of bud-burst beech leaves in the spring,
Red of rhus and cherry in the fall,
The blue of harebells on the roadside hedge,
Smiling eyes gazing into mine,
Sky-blue, content.
These I have loved.
W P Kneen

Lifeboat and Station
Fishermen alerted by boy's beating drum,
'Come along Brave boys, come along.'
Fishermen altered by firing of a gun from Formby Shore.

Two fishing villages North East and North West.
Bound both by a humane and selfless quest.
The recovery of persons drowning at sea.

On horseback in the teeth of the gale they tore.
Be it to Redcar or to Formby beach.
Lifeboat men their stations would reach.
Each man a volunteer.

Horses hooked to carriage of lifeboat
Dragging their load along the beach.
To reach the best place to cross the raging foam
And let the crew bring souls in distress
To safe harbour home.

Those horses would enter the water deep,
Till the boat pulled clear and faced the gale
That made men tie themselves to the mast.
In a Vessel fast breaking in the storm.
And sounding a horn, eerie, and forlorn.
A cry in the night, hope kept alive.
By the lighthouse light and the sight
Of the lifeboat men.

Formby the first lifeboat station in the land.
Redcar, the Zetland oldest lifeboat in the world.
Freda Grieve

My Mum's Trip to the Palace
They came from afar to visit Buck House,
and as usual along came a coach load of scouse.

My mum was on that trip to the palace,
she met Americans who thought it was just like Dallas.

She stayed in a hotel and visited the sights,
a taxi ride took her to those wonderful delights.

Screaming Lord Sutch was visiting too,
dressed as usual like no others do.

What's all the fuss about visiting the palace for a fee,
when you can visit my house and it's for free!

Eight pounds to get in was the price they paid,
cor blimey that money would buy me loads of sweets and lemonade.

My mum grabbed a photographer as she boarded the bus,
she said, 'Hey mate how about a photo of the four of us.'

My mum, nanna cat, and nanna and grandad, Henry too,
all of them waving and off to see you know who.

She loved it so much, she can't wait to go again,
next time she will be wanting to appear on News at Ten!
Brian Dougan

A Holiday of a Lifetime!
Fasten your seat belts,
Keep seated until we're in the sky.
Be prepared for the holiday of a lifetime!
Attention please
This is a nine hour journey,
Undo your seat belts,
Drinks are being served.

The heat hit me
At the top of the plane steps.
It whooshed up my skirt
But I was here!
Florida -
Land of sun and fun.

Where shall we go first?
Disney Land?
Sea World?
Epcot Centre?

There's so much to choose from.
The atmosphere is hot and exciting,
I love it.

The sun finds every hiding place,
A ball of fire
Reflecting on the sea.
There's Minnie Mouse
Thunder Mountain
Peter Pan.
Kennedy Space Centre,
Hot and heavy from the sun.
I remember it all
As if it was yesterday.
Hannah Melling (10)

Memories of Pendle Hill
Dear old Pendle, we see thee
slumbering 'neath the setting sun.
You will still be there for countless years,
When our short race is run.

The weary traveller, homeward bound,
breathes a grateful sigh,
When he sees thee in the distance,
His journey's end is nigh.

We strolled along your ways,
When we were in our prime.
Enjoying all your changing moods
We seemed to find the time.

The lowering rain swept clouds of sky
Obscure you from our view
But with the dawn of another day
The sun will shine on you.

So slumber on our dear old hill
We no longer stroll your ways.
But we shall still remember you,
From wonderful happier days.
Mary Halsall

Happenings
The wind is high on Pendle Hill,
But eerily, all the trees are still.
The melting darkness of the night,
Hides the witches in their flight.

To their meeting place they fly,
Under shade of the darkened sky.
Hooded cloaks cover their faces,
Broomsticks whisk them to far off places.

Picking herbs to create their spells,
Over hill and down the dells.
Making ointment, creams and lotions,
Concocting strange and wonderful potions.

Returning home before it gets light,
Flying through what is left of the night.
Arriving back safely on Pendle Hill,
Where all the trees are eerily still.

To their beds they now must creep,
Catching up on precious sleep.
Until the night falls once again,
Once more to collect their precious bane.
Gwen Walsh

My Isle
Where the greenest grass grows,
And the purest stream flows.
Ellan Vannin, my isle,
To my face brings a smile.
In the blue Irish sea,
The land of the free.
My dearest dwell here,
Where the air's pure and clear.
In Snaefells' shadow dark,
The moors lie stark.
The lonely Curlew cries,
Beneath the overcast skies.
Then as if in a dream,
The sun begins to beam.
Gone is the gloom,
Now gorse and heather bloom.
The snow and the blow,
The heat and sun's glow,
In all its changing face,
Eilan Vannin shows grace.
Wherever I roam
Ellan Vannin is my home.
Shelley Walker (13)

Big Ben
Not one face, this one
Not two, or four
A face for any season
Any day
Or time of day . . .
Ben More,

It dominates the glen
Not Westminster
Its hands, not large or small
But finger strands
Of snow
Long after the last fall.

It strikes no hours
It has but one -
Timeless: Yet on its slopes
Are ever changing shadows
Day - long
From the sun.

No busyness surrounds it
The Great Hill
Since the last granite upheaval
Keeping its own counsel
Silent
Still.

It tells you not how early you will be
When you must rush about
Or late -
But you may learn the wisdom of the ages
If you will watch this mute Big Ben . . .
And wait.
David Batten

Rural Tayside
No horse's hoofprints mark the soil
Just a deep tyre tread today,
No straining muscles of pure delight
Technology now holds sway.

But progress means so many things
No voice of command, no creaking chains,
Just a huge powerful machine steered by
Hands on the wheel, which never held reins.

So the food mountains grow while the wildlife recedes
Till the cycle turns right 'round,
Now it's less production, put back those hedges
Plant trees on that bare ground.

Yet through all this the scene remains
The high mountains, the lochs and glens,
The purple moors and the forests green
Nothing as flat as the fens.

Now this is what the tourists seek
They come and view and see,
And find some peace and enchantment
Therefore this is the place for me.
Donald McKerchar

The Meaning of Strathclyde
Living here within Strathclyde
Means quite a lot to me,
There are various entertainments
For all to come and see.
Chatelherault and Strathclyde Park
The racecourse and the skating
The library the town hall too
They all have first class rating!

Of course it's Hamilton of which I'm proud
As it's here that I reside
Being a mature student with ambition
Where better than Strathclyde?

To fulfil the dreams I once let slip
Bell college I'm attending
With support from Strathclyde Region
My education is ascending!

And so towards the leisure side of the town I call my home
Hamilton point is the place to go should you care to roam,
Seen as the best on a social scale
It's the *in spot* known to all
For when inside its plush surroundings
Your sure to have a ball!

Going further afield to East Kilbride
With its fancy shops galore
With the malls inside that are all enclosed
Outside the rain can pour!

With regards to Motherwell the town right next to mine
There's the bowling and the Aquatec to take up leisure time
But all in all its only part of Strathclyde regions cream
And I'm sure that in the future new ventures they'll be seen,
To enhance the lives of young and old disabled people too
By introducing many schemes whether they be old or new!
So to finish of this attribute
All I have left to say
Is I wish the region all the best
Today and everyday!
Maureen Egan

The Doctor's Surgery
I'm sitting in a place filled with bacteria
Filled with depression and malignant hysteria
My nerves are shattered, I'm filled with pain
I'm sat in my doctor's surgery again.

I didn't feel to bad when I entered the door.
Then I thought of my pain, *oh it's really sore.*
I didn't get much sleep last night
Just look at those children starting to fight!

I've got funny sensations from top to toe
And a funny lump that's starting to grow.
I've backache headache and a pain in my side
And a clonking hip that hurts when I stride.

I've palpitations, paranoiac thinking
I'm sure the water's not right that I've been drinking
I'm not to sure of the tablets I've been taking
I'm sweating a lot and violently shaking.

Mind you I think I might be first getting a cold
Or then again I might be getting old,
Oh dear, it's the red light - it's me!
I'll have to pay for my prescription fee.

Now I seem to have forgotten what I've come for
His name's looking at me on the big black door.
I think I'll not bother telling him a thing
When I get home I'll give him a ring!
Iris Grice

Race Day
Sunrise creeping, daylight peeping,
All is silent, all are sleeping.

Stables stirring, clocks a-whirring,
Farm dogs scratching, farm cats purring;

Voices rising, (some surmising)
Scent of coffee - appetising;

Harness jingling, senses tingling,
Smell of sweat and horse breath mingling;

Boxes ready - hold 'em steady!
Even now they're feeling heady;

Race-day thrilling, people milling,
Horses happy, keen and willing;

Crowds a-growing, to and fro-ing,
Winning stables proudly crowing;

Steeds parading, promenading,
Hopes increasing, chances fading;

Expectation, presentation,
High excitement, rich sensation;

A miracle happens, it's a winner,
Paying for champagne and dinner;

Horses fed now, put to bed now,
Long before the weary tread now;

Happy voices, early morning -
Soon to rise again at dawning;

Sunrise creeping, daylight peeping,
All is silent, all are sleeping . . .
Mark Newberry

Looking After the Land
I praise and thank God, for this wonderful land,
Created and moulded by his mighty hand,
The beauty surrounding us we can see,
In a gift freely given to you and to me.

All the fells and the mountains that look to the sky,
And the rivers and streams full of water flow by,
The grass, the flowers their foliage green,
Spread over the earth in beauty serene.

The sun in the summer its warm glow to cheer,
The snow and the wind tell us winter is here,
Creatures with new born herald the springtime,
The trees in the autumn their colours divine.

But what can we do to keep it this way,
So beauty is here for now and always,
We need to be taught to care for all things,
And we would enjoy all that life brings.

Then ever we eat out of packets or tins,
We should make sure rubbish goes into bins,
And when we have drunk our orange or coke,
Not to throw it in fields where cattle could choke.

When we go to the country, a trip from town,
And after our picnic don't throw litter down,
Then the fields and parks wherever we roam,
Would stay fresh and clean 'cause we took litter home.
Phyllis Carpenter

Untitled
October in the wee country
Today the trees are yellow
and green. The Boughs hanging
little green grapes and when
the winter sun shines bright
the trees turn to gold in the
wee country.
Margaret Dewar

The Squirrel

Little squirrel grey and brown,
Like the leaves all around,
Babbling like the hidden brook,
Till you've found a sheltered nook,
Up a tree with shining bark,
To hide away until it's dark.
Friendly the sound of a human voice,
The scent of a dog, you have no choice,
Safe in the trees with the wind and the sun,
My spirit you've lifted, my heart you have won.
Till one day I see you lying,
On the roadside torn and dying,
Blooded breast 'twas once so white,
With softest fur and eyes alight
Ne'er see the day nor yet the night.
Betty Samson

September Fires

Late evening and a light wind
Sends farmers burning straw in harvest fields.
From where I stand, warm in an anorak,
I see dancing coronas, flickering gold,
Releasing smoke, the colour of sunsets,
To drift and rise into
A egg shell sky.

There, beneath the hills,
A castle flares in light - is gone!
Towards the east, the three-pronged dovecote,
Centuries old, stands out in black relief.
Fires expand space, an optical illusion,
But viewed form higher ground
It must look as though
The cities of the plains are burning.

Beside me, the apple orchard
Holds in her dark green breath -
Daring the long sierras of fire
To come much closer;
The top of the oak tree glows with light
And farm house chimneys blush and pale again.

Tonight, fantastic movement, flame-red energy,
Tomorrow, stillness and the black scorched earth
Cleaned and ready to take new seed
In whose dark cells . . .

Lie the germ
Of their own destruction.
Margaret Gilles-Brown

Barbados Holiday
'Neath tropic sun, the noonday gun, is signal for siesta.
As night descends, you make amends, by joining in fiesta.
Drink fiery rum, distilled from cane
Come sunrise, oh the ache, the pain
Make vows of never, never again.

On sandy beach, just out of reach, of wavelets in profusion.
Your body glows, as you repose in sunshine and seclusion.
The temperate sea, reflecting sky
Like a siren calls, come hie, come hie
Swim to the reef if you dare to try.

But days wear on, times soon come, when spirits are a yearning.
Adieus are said, arrangements made, for homewards returning.
The aircraft waits, crew at ease
Fasten seat belts, no smoking please
Farewell Barbados, Carribean seas.
Derek Fellows

The Hustler
'Twas on the Broads of Norfolk
In the autumn of the year,
That I met a certain hustler
And unto her drew near.
Sometime a slow, quiet, gentle thing,
Sometime a busy bustler,
On the Norfolk plain, midst wind and rain
I fell for the charms of the hustler.

We travelled all the daylight hours
Then by the water's edge we rested
On the waters wide, barely swept by the tide
Where the grebe and the heron nested.
Sometime in sun and calm and quiet
Then rain . . . wind strong and gustier.
As we shared the rivers, cuts and broads
I fell in love with the hustler.

It's near a year since last I saw her
Since then, many others have had her.
But I'll see her again, sun, wind or rain
And we'll share again that rapture.
I'll meet her in shyness,
She'll accept me in patience.
But I long for the day, and it's not far away
When I hoist up the sails of the Hustler.
Ray Ashworth

Reluctant Traveller
I seldom wish to go away
In search of sun that shines all day,
Or yearn for sounds of far off lands,
For desert islands, sea and sands.

The wall of China holds no charms,
Bangkok, Hong Kong or waving palms
Along the beach of Agadir -
Well, maybe I could go next year . . .

But sometimes one must venture far,
By plane or boat, but mostly car,
To visit friends and those held dear
Meeting at venues far and near.

'It's nice to have a change,' they say
And may we'll return one day,
But it's wonderful to go back home
With cases packed - no more to roam.

And my spirits always rise,
Be there sun or leaden skies,
When Kendal and The Lakes appear
On Motorway signs - and Windermre.

Why did I ever go away?
Especially in the month of May,
It's always so good to come back
 . . . to Witherslack.
Trish Johnson

Breakfast With Ducks on The River Lune - West Bank
Step warily as you descend Mill Brow
The robins will keep you company
Such music helps somehow.

On the bank pause and think
What scents pervade the air,
Herbs of fennel and aniseed,
Grasses, varied, tall and fair

Along the edge a family grows
Of maple or English asa
Shoulder high, as the river flows
Smooth and gentle rippleless water.

Rich are the trees on every side
In multi-colours and shade
Reflections, broken, causing divide
Confluence, disturbance made.

Being alert and no one near
A white chested dipper
May bobbingly appear
Then swiftly dip and disappear.

The ancient heavy fallen oak
New shedding its serrated leaves
Stands determined to hold its own
Eternal, mistakenly believes.

The Devil's Bridge, my happy goal
Is here, all too soon -
With slices of bread, or whole

Happy ducks, just like me
Enjoy their breakfast treat
Always a glorious sight to see
Fighting beak to beak.
Iris Robertson

Pride and Prejudice
I tried my best to lure her
as she toured the Golden Mile:
I tried my best to tempt her
with my polished, sparkling smile.

I knew that I could please her
if she came into my bed.
I knew that she'd be happy,
contented and well fed.

I watched as she came nearer
and looked me up and down:
I watched for her reaction -
would she smile or would she frown?

Her hand reached out to touch me,
my pride began to swell -
Her hand was edging nearer -
come on lady, ring my bell!

She came in with her suitcase
and laid it on my bed:
She came in with her daughter
her son, and husband, Ted.

A guest house, proud and busy
is what I am, you see.
A credit to the Nation
at Blackpool-by-the-sea.
Ruth Maria Midgley

Between the Passes
Hidden in the valley
Snuggled down
Like a chick in its nest,
If only my arms would stretch
To caress
The shoulders of these stooping giants.
But I am just a speck
If spied from 'top those hills

Yet my eyes are blessed
To draw the panoramic view within-
to etch and sketch the contours
Of rounded moss and bracken fells
The green; grey and black crags and rocks
With weals and welts,
Boulders balanced;
Precariously placed.
To flick through these pictures in my mind
At any time
What a wondrous gift - serene, sublime
To experience, in the depths,
Breathtaking elation
Gazing up to the heights of this
mountainous creation.
Gill Pickup

Double Dutch
Hurry hurry to the station
Bags in hand
In anticipation,
To a land
Across the water
Is my final destination.
Will the journey be a good one
Will the sea be calm and still
If it's rough aboard the ferry
I hope I won't be sick or ill,
Stood in deck I watch the spray
It's so good to get away
To a land of clogs and cheeses
Happy faces, hugs and squeezes.
Tulips as far as the eye can see
This truly is the place to be
In the springtime or the fall
I love Holland best of all.
Elizabeth Thorpe

Remembrance Day
We have come to remember our nation's dead
And we wear our poppies with pride
As we pause for a moment or two to recall
The men and the women who've died,
In wars that no one has truly won
At a cost we must never forget.
But as we stand with our heads bowed in silence
The wars are continuing yet.
For the guns and the bombs are not silenced
And the poppies will bloom just as red
When the people of Enniskillen
Pause to remember their dead.
A C Brennan

My Cottage
In a picturesque setting of hill and dale,
Tucked away, in a grassy vale,
I know some day there will be,
A sweet country cottage just for me.

With walls of white and a roof of thatch
Inside would be nice and neat,
Log fire in the hearth, for warm and cosy heat,
Firelight flickering on the windows at night.

A beautiful garden with a fence all around,
Peaceful and quiet,
The honeybee buzzing and the nightingales song
is the only sound,
you would hear when you come along.

In a cosy chair, there I would sit,
Watching the birds,
A robin, a sparrow,
a chaffinch and a blue-tit.

They would visit the bird table,
looking for a tasty dish,
next to the pond,
where there's plenty of fish.

There would be
Roses around the door
Who could ask for more,
When I'm old this is my wish.
Marion Talbot

Greetings on Meetings
An American will say,
Have a nice day,
Meaning don't get mugged or shot.
Australians greet,
With 'G day mate,'
And Castlemaine XXXX when it's hot.
A Frenchman may say, 'Bonjour,'
The farmers Baa English lamb.
The Vatican claims the word of God,
Argentina just the hand.
British greetings vary,
From North, South, East or West,
But being a Northerner, I find,
'Hello Luv,' just the best.
Then, 'What about this weather?'
Someone is sure to say;
It's all so very easy,
It changes from day to day.
Women talk of the price of meat,
And the bargains in the sale;
While men talk about *that* team,
And the referee who's blind.
'I don't know why I watch them,
They go from bad to worse;

'But are you going Saturday?'
'See you there, of course.'
'Where has all the time gone,
We'll really have to rush,
Give our love to one and all,
We've enjoyed our talk so much.'
G Rowe

River Holiday
There are boats of different kinds
on each joining river,
In and out as water winds,
seemingly forever.

Little boats for two or three,
Easy for the moorings,
Others large for family,
making swells a soaring.

Ducks and coots with chicks in tow,
Hoping for some food,
Whether tides are high or low,
We can see their brood.

The swans sail by in regal way,
Each one with a mate,
They stay together day by day,
Unless they part by fate.

We see a heron standing still,
on a post longside,
With head held high and a long bill,
Watching waters glide.

The reeds and rivers team with life,
Although there is such peace,
'Tis restful for each busy wife,
Where noise of towns do cease.

There are always willing hands,
To help us when we moor,
Fellow boaters, no demands,
Pull the ropes ashore.

We stop at village stores for food,
And wander down the lanes,
And then return in happy mood,
As the sunset wanes.
Winifred Woolfelden

A Song of Surrey
I sing a song of the Surrey hills
tender and green and kind.
Gorse bloom gleams gold in the summer sun
a singing skylark climbs high in the sky,
blue shadows fall as the evening comes,
and in the woods on the slopes shy deer stand,
silent among the trees.

I sing a song of the old Surrey lanes
quiet and secret and hidden.
Still there despite new death-ridden roads.
Violets in spring, roses and honeysuckle in summer,
Autumn hedges trailing with traveller's joy and berries,
dusty in summer, a carpet of leaves in autumn
crackling under the feet.

I sing a song of the old Surrey names,
the *folds* and *fords*, the *hams* the *bury's*
villages and inns and small country churches.
Saxon and Dane, Roman and Norman
they all left their mark on people and places.
Fields where old battles raged, causes were lost,
dead men lie buried.

I sing a song of Surrey, my home.
soft airs and cool summer breezes.
Strong autumn gales, cold winter winds.
The old Surrey people were gentle and wise,
they have knowledge of strange things from the past.
The hills, the lanes, the wise gentle people,
all this is Surrey.
Marge A Chamberlain

Gargoyle
The bird on the wall
Was seduced by the call
While the gargoyles watched from above.
It heard the children's screams
As they played out all their dreams
Wrapped safely in their mother's love.

But the gargoyles grew wise
As they listened to the lies
That were poured into innocent ears
And the bird flew away
As the children ceased to play
And were trapped into falsehoods and fears.

With arrogance they grew
They believed it through and through
That life was a game they could win
But as the walls came tumbling down
And the children began to drown
The gargoyles suppressed a grin.

With bitterness installed
Life no more enthralled
And alcohol replaced all their dreams
And in a drunken haze
They played out all their days
And silently suppressed the screams.

But the bird on the wall
Was seduced by the call
While the gargoyles laughed in the skies
it heard the children's screams
As they played out all their dreams
And listened to their mother's lies.
Talitha Tallett

Sunday Bus
Sunday morning and waiting, for one more bus,
In empty, sound - and - soulless station.
The shops shuttered with graffiti-daubed, grey steel,
And no one there waiting
But the one, that is the only number that counts
In the games that losers play.

Kick, for knowing, the bag lying
Not so casual at scuffed feet.
Holding the careless stuffed clothes that
Cocoon, the careful placed, soon needed bottle
The holding all, holdall.
To be tossed, with feigned indifference, on the bus
That is fear-filled certain not to come.

And yet this, the lesser fear.
For the sick, nameless dread of the uncertain tortures
The not yet, yet certain rejection, waiting, endlessly rehashed.
This distorts reason, agitates and flutters strong
In churning, unquiet gut.
Joe Heeley

Solace
I went to the hills in my loneliness
there to seek solace from pain.
But all I found in the wilderness
was the wind and the endless rain.

I walked through fields and heather
Braving the cold and storm,
Knowing for me, there never would
be - a fire to keep me warm.

I went to the hills with my sorrow
And there left my tears and sighs,
I went to the hills in my loneliness
The wind dried the tears in my eyes.
Dorris Braithwaite

Untitled
The posters said to get ahead to England you
must come.
This land of hope and glory welcomes everyone.
In the dark a lone dog bark seldom see the sun.
To cut and hue and make things new you
always have to run.

Strange faces that you meet each day come
from worlds apart.
No palm trees no coconut. No porcelain in the still.
No mountains of green valleys, no cottage
on the hill.
Nonetheless without much rest. To stay a
while I will.

Strangers speak in native tongue there is
out and nought. I am mystified.
Buildings all in rubble left over from the
blitz, I was not expecting this.
Commitment on the faces of all the confused
races.
To build a nest is no jest ambition is
so gracious.

Lonely as the days go by on thoughts
of home, I sometimes sit and cry.
Tears soon dry and with a sigh nostalgia
fades away.
No time to pray just toil each day from
morn' to evening sun.
But then again, I guess that's why I come.
M McKenna

Morecambe Bay - Flookburgh Fishermen
Eat your heart out puny paddler
As you cockle in the bay
And a tractor out of Flookburgh clamours by:
A chariot of glory
With its rainbowed wings of spray
And an oily-clad Elijah riding high.
The sodden steppes of sweeping sand,
The serpent channels' glint,
Reflect a subtle tapestry of light:
From hazy dawn's awaking
In a blaze of kindling tints,
To pewtered rose as evening shades to night.

Eat your heart out puny paddler
As you flee the tidal bore
And you dream of wheels to speed you on your way.
Be grateful that you've seen it:
And the dying breed of men
Who cajole a grudging living from the bay.
Freda Bunce

Come to Sunny Bowdon
Come to sunny Bowdon
The experts proudly say
There's Minor County cricket
Watch the cream of Devon play.

The cricket will be thrilling
No cloud up in the sky
With bat and ball in combat
As the breeze blows gently by.

With Cheshire on a *Flyer*
And Devon in full flow
Exciting entertainment
Will make the tension grow.

There's Miller and there's Roebuck
To prove that class will out
One with cunning bowling
The other with some *clout*.

And so the crowd did gather
But the weather, it was grey
And the umpires said those dreaded words
'There won't be any play.'
Tony Sheldon

On a Pennine Hill
When I stand upon some hilltop
Where the wind blows strong and free,
With the rugged moorlands beauty
Spreading far in front of me.
Then I think of men before me,
Of another day and age,
Singing praises through their poetry,
To our Northern heritage.

What would I give to put my thoughts
In words, as did those gifted men,
For I would let my spirit speak
Out through the medium of my pen.
Eric Johnson

The Revenant
When I used to live in Lees,
Everything was just as you please.
But I always wanted to live in Grotton,
Away from the touch of cotton,
Or even in Uppermill,
With a flower box on the windowsill.
But this thing never happened,
Even so my heart was gladdened,
I moved away from Lancashire,
To Ilkeston in Derbyshire.
But I kept returning to Lees,
Where I had learned about the birds and bees.
I could never settle anywhere,
My life was lived in complete despair.
I should have spent my life,
Away from all this trouble and strife,
In Lees, yes in Lees,
Where everything was just as you please.
Now I live in Penwortham,
Where they don't say eeh by gum.
I have lived here for fifteen years,
What shall I do? Give three cheers.
Dorothy Hilditch

The Caterpillar
There was a baby caterpillar who crawled out from an egg,
She looked around the cabbage patch, 'What lovely food,' she said.
She lived upon a cabbage leaf. Her family all around,
She ate and ate from dawn till dusk and never made a sound.

She grew big and fat from all that food till she could eat no more.
She crawled along the garden path and in through the shed door.
She found herself a comfy place in which to go to bed.
A chrysalis formed 'round her from her tail up to her head.

All through winter she stayed there: for months she slept and slept,
Then one hot day the sun shone in and from her cocoon she crept.
First her head, and then the rest all suddenly appeared,
She really was quite sleepy still as 'round the shed she peered.

She lay quite still for a short while, the sun shone on her back.
She thought she'd go out for a walk but found she'd lost the knack.
She tried to walk a little way, she looked down at her feet.
And then she saw that she had wings, so pretty and so neat.

She stretched her wings, so clean and new in colours oh so bright,
With spots of red and dots of blue and patches of pure white.
As she spread her wings, she flew outside, towards the sky,
Oh what a glorious thing to be,
                      a beautiful butterfly!
Rosemary Atherton

Animals
Some animals are gentle and kind,
In the light the mole is blind.
The hedgehog spiky, the rabbit soft,
And the little mice in your loft.
Owls fly high in the midnight sky,
In the fields below the horses lie.
All these animals should be okay,
But some are killed every day.
Why do people do things like this,
Because all the animals we will miss.
Hayley Fairhurst (9)

The Four Seasons
In spring the snowdrop starts to bloom,
And buds and plants begin to grow
While all the trees still look so gloom
Where rivers and streams steadily flow.

Oh wonderful spring
What a beautiful start
To a brand new season
The happiest at heart.

In summertime the sun shines high
And beautiful flowers burst with colours bright
With melting ice - creams, a sun filled sky
Sandy beaches and the long cool nights.

Oh wonderful summer
The beauty of the sun
The trees, the flowers, the fruit
And all that is much fun.

At autumn time leaves fall from the trees,
And wither with the whispering breeze,
All scattered here and everywhere
They gather together in piles so rare!

Oh wonderful autumn
The trees now bare
The colder days
The winds that don't care.

At wintertime the snow falls down
The snowflakes twirl 'round and 'round
Falling down around the town
They whish and whirl without a sound.

Oh wonderful winter
Beautiful and white,
The lovely scenery
So magnificent and bright!
Debbie L McGrory

Summer Solstice
Sky open to the fields.
Hay lying to dry.
River glittering in the sun.
Sticky, sleepy day.
At highest point,
Then sun sinks to rest.
Zoë Turpin

What a Wonderful Thing a Flower
A seed one does sow,
From seed the flower does grow,
A wonderful sight to see,
Reproductive organs work magically.

Some flowers are very small,
Others are extremely tall,
The scents are really beautiful,
One never forgets them at all.

In parks are patterns worked with flowers,
In gardens people plant away for hours,
The reward in the end really gives pleasure,
Walking by. Going to work. Or at leisure.

The variety of colours in the many flowers,
Brightens up the days, minutes. The hours.
They give pleasure to everyone,
They thrive with rain and sun.

If given when one is ill,
They can work magic. As good as a pill.
As a gift one cannot be wrong.
Flowers can give a lift as does a song.

A flower is a symbol of love,
As a symbol of peace is a dove,
They work wonders all around the world,
From minute buds, till petals are fully uncurled.

A flower is around in any season,
There to give for any reason,
Without them where would we be,
They always make people happy.
J Dormer

Seasons
The autumn leaves are falling down,
Making a carpet of golden brown.
All shining with dew, and pretty too,
Like a lovely picture, like a sky of blue.

Winter we know is on the way,
The nights are dark at the end of day.
Curtains are drawn, the lamp lights glisten,
We sit round the fire, to stories listen.

The wind may howl, and dogs may bark,
Birds have flown, no song from the lark.
Alas let autumn have its way,
Our life goes on from day to day.

We must be thankful for each season,
Spring brings the lambs, the flowers as well,
Summer brings sunshine in which we dwell.
Autumn is lovely with the leaves of gold,
Then comes winter with the ice and cold.
The seasons come, the seasons go,
But life goes on for ever.
Melda Larsen

Autumn

Oh autumn, beautiful autumn,
Your colours are supreme
Your trees have changed from green
To a beauty so lovely and serene.
And soon you shed your leaves
Like petals falling in the wind
To make a carpet for all mankind.

Oh autumn, beautiful autumn,
Don't undress your trees too soon,
We love your leaves up there
On branches that look up to the moon.
Your swaying and rustlings your
Whispering and nodding.
Your families of birds and squirrels,
Nesting there.

Oh autumn, beautiful autumn,
When all your leaves have gone
And scattered everywhere,
We hope that they will find
Their place to grow again next year.
Catherine Butterworth

Autumn

The autumn leaves fall to the
ground, their colour red and gold.
But some are still a bit green,
Walk into the woods and see,
All the glories of the trees,
And the ground covered with
different coloured leaves,
And the autumn colour of the skies.
Seemed to be just as nice as
the leaves on the ground.

Where there's different colours all around,
Autumn likes to show her colour
Because there isn't any there.
Probably summer's second best,
But autumn is at her best,
Wherever you may wander,
Wherever you may roam,
England is more founder,
Of autumn's red and gold,
You cannot beat autumn's light,
When the evening is near the night.
Pretty colours you will find in
Autumn's day and evening light.
Rose Hoskins

Untitled
The wind is wild
It seems to talk
of age and time.
The sea and wine
wilder the wind blows
more fickle the weather
as we stroll
arm in arm together.
Playfully winds blow
down to the sea
without a thought
for you and me.
But wilder still, is,
talk without deeds
so often we ignore
each other's needs
Though wild the wind
like many a race
let us all try
to withstand the pace.
Millicent Sinclair

The Star
The star shone bright in the sky that night,
That night so long ago,
When a child was born in Bethlehem,
In a stable humble, and low.
And shepherds came from the fields to see,
to kneel in wonder, and pray,
Led by the star which shone so bright,
to the stable where Jesus lay.
And wise men came from distant lands,
with incense, gold and myrrh,
guided by that shining star,
as Jesus lay sleeping there.
And we would do well to remember,
the cry of the shepherds then.
Glory to God in the Highest,
On earth Peace and Goodwill to all men.
Lily Alyward

Leaves
Overhead they fly and camp down on the floor
And you seated by the courtyard
Whereupon the winds shuffle up them all,
A grass so green but now made crisp
Beside the leaves that lay and sift
And as my thoughts sift through the sky
Of the world your on when you go on by.

Sycamores, chestnuts take up the room left bare
Soon they have nowhere to go
And the ones left out stay in the air.
A pair of people hold hands in bliss
And on the leaves they lay and kiss
Each surrendered now to their lovers eyes
As they share together the clouded night.

You and I are the land that stretches beyond
Let me take you to the kingfisher
That's the one that lives beside the pond,
And on the ground I make new space
To support your soul and all your weight
And leave the ponds edge clean and dry
Fly the kingfisher with you to the sky.

Dandelions, magpies towards my right sail by
Our time is near as clouds set in
And darkness covers up the night
Building rafts we sail across the lake
Doing our best to stay awake
Burn it when we get to the other side
As we see the stars lighten up the sky.

Rodger Moir

Lakeland Speaks
I am proud of myself; I have been here for years.
I boast pretty villages, thick forests and meres.
My memories go back to days when only wild beasts
And ancient man scratched my surface for frugal feasts.

Through the thousands of springs I have witnessed the leaves
Open their glory; The valley grass gently heaves
To and fro in the summer sun, then dies as the chill
Of autumn and winter fills the valleys and crowns the hill.

Yes, I am proud of myself, my beauty has inspired
Artists, naturalists, climbers and poets; I am desired
By seekers of peace and by convalescents for pure air
That makes them light-headed. I warn you, beware!

Yes, beware you don't abuse me and render me ill,
Poison my air and let death my lungs fill.
I am God's gift to the people of this land
Not a dump where the world's rubbish can disband.
Elizabeth Monaghan

Eventide
One evening as I sat alone, I raised my questing eye,
and watched the first faint star appear above me, in the sky.

I lingered in my solitude, at the coming of the night,
till high up in the heavens shone a million points of light,
and I heaved a thankful sigh, that at last the job was done.
That the daily strain was over, and the struggle had been won.

I looked again at the firmament, that vast eternity,
where now a brightly shining moon rose up majestically,
and in that cool clear evening its ghostly silver light
shone down on me as I sat there, in the quiet of the night,
while my tender nether regions felt the obvious, draughty proof,
that an old style outside privy's mighty cold without a roof.
J R Arrowsmith

Snowing
When you wake in
the morning
it's snowing.
You're yawning
and bed is
a haven of warmth.
Then the cold wind
starts biting,
and nipping and
lighting your cheeks.
When your nose
has gone purple,
and the wind is
intolerable.
And your Christmas
wish is for
winter to cease.

One day before
long;
Winter will have gone.
And you will be
left in some
peace.
Alexander Southgate (12)

The Harvest Moon
Oh! Harvest moon how thou doth shine,
With a deep golden glow all so divine.
As I gaze at thee from my window,
I am enraptured by thy Heavenly glow.
Having risen from above Gorple moor,
Higher and higher into the sky thou doth soar,
As thou wilt do now and forever more.
No wonder thou art worshipped by man,
With thy infinite glorious eternal lifespan.
Long may thou beam that radiant glow,
Down upon us poor mortals here far below.
To inspire us all forever more.
To think that man has trod on thy shore,
He must have felt close to heaven's door.
Seeing our Earth revolving in space,
In all of its glory and mystical grace.
What a wonderful sight to look down and face,
He said he felt nearer to Heaven then,
Having reached heights unseen by other men.
Man may seek other planets to explore,
But thy lovely face no one can ignore.
For amidst that infinite starry galaxy,
In total command thou wilt ever be,
Guiding everyone safely to their destiny,
Whether on the land air or sea.
Brian Watson

My Tree
Once in my garden stood a beautiful tree,
I watched it grow up with my family.
It grew so tall and green and wide,
Birds sang in its branches, and there breezes sighed.
I loved that tree, and now it is hewed,
With only a stump, to show where it stood.
I weep for the loss of that beautiful tree,
And grieve as if it were family.
I look out of my window, and all I see,
Is a stark empty space, where once stood a tree.
Jennie Doran

The Field
This ground was here before we came
Each furrow tossed and turned,
And so were all the natural things
Like pits and birds and worms.

This brook has flowed for many a year
And drenched the celendine,
And been a home for tiny fish
Who paddle to its rhyme.

This tree has stood against the wind
And sheltered many a bird,
Who nest within its lofty boughs
Their choicest songs have heard.

This pond with pussy willow graced
And reeds upon the bank,
Here all the little tadpoles play
The shallow end is dank.

This cop has held a sweet bouquet
Of dandelion spray,
The foxglove and the wild bluebell
Oh spring! Prolong your stay.

This dew is fresh upon the grass
The silver mist of dawn,
Will ride upon the skylark's wing
To greet the sunny morn'.
Annie Harrison

End of Another Year
The falling leaf
The dark'ning sky
Winter is coming by and by,
Winter is coming.

A sob of the wind
The sleet and snow.
And the little robin as nowhere to go.
He sits and sings from up the tree.
To let us know it's thee end of the year.
A Woodcock

Autumn
Autumn time is fun,
There's never any time to be glum,
Red and gold leaves,
Fall off the trees,
So there's no excuse to be glum.

Autumn time is fun,
So you go and tell your mum,
She might let you play,
And she might make you stay,
So try to be good,
And stay out of that *mud!*

Georgina Gorton (11)

The Robin
Down in the valley, white with snow
Hardly a blade of grass does show
Powdery flakes flutter down to rest
Ah' here comes a little Robin Redbreast,

He looks at the window with a cheeky eye
And seems to say, 'When will you feed I?'
I hurry out with some crumbs of bread
And he thanks me with a nod of his head.

'Oh, Mr Robin, can you tell me please
When will this wintry weather cease,
When will the snowdrops and crocus bloom?
Ah, I see you have eaten every last crumb.'

Off he flew with a twitch of his tail
He'll be back tomorrow, without fail
My feathered friends brighten up my day
I hope they will always fly my way.

When the snow has gone, and grass is green
The birds in my garden will still be seen
In the branches of the apple tree
Singing and chirping so merrily.
G E Cannell

Contrasts
Rainswept streets
Bared to the angry sky,
Regular grey-bricked edifices,
Shuttered, rollered, as to die,
And litter, a gust sweeps,
And only the gulls' mournful cry.

Streets baked dry
By a burning, cruel sun,
And packed, life rushing by,
Time for no man,
Nor even a gentle sigh,
And traffic, madly, comes, goes, but nev'r is gone.

Rain-drenched fields,
Savaged by angry clouds,
And hills scourged by thundery peals.
Long, since they blossomed proud.
A solitary gull wheels,
And glides, and wheels again around.

Ripening corn
Waving in the gentle breeze,
Signalling a new day's morn',
And garlanded leas
Cradling lambs newly-born,
And nestling, open-mouthed, in the trees.
Anthony Smith

Nature and Spring
As I walk down a country lane thinking of the past
The world has changed, and troubles cast.
But nature and growth remain the same
A thrush is singing, perched on chimney high
The sun is shining, there's a clear blue sky.
A startled bird flies from its nest
As I look, it's a robin red breast
Blackbird calling to its mate,
That's perching on the farmyard gate.
Cattle in the fields are grazing
A cockerel crows, a horse starts naying
The cow's are waiting to be milked
A farmer comes to guide them in,

As I walk and see these things
My heart gives just a little twinge
Nature and love, they are a beautiful thing
We feel this most, with the approach of spring
Flowers bloom, bees pollinate the various plants
This is the time that nature calls
When born are creatures, great and small.
Eileen D Shaw

Ideal Home
Her house is a show-house
Nothing out of place.
Matching cushions and curtains
In exquisite taste.
Dainty porcelain figures
On highly-polished wood,
Cut-glass sparkles in sunlight,
Exactly as it should.

Uncluttered kitchen work-tops
Not a pan in sight.
Dried flowers and Chinese cook books -
A culinary delight.
The garden's an explosion of colour,
The lawn's a bowling green.
The bathroom's like something from *Ideal Home*
And she's the cul-de-sac queen!

The bedroom's all frilly in peaches,
The curtains - all swaggers and tails
She's slim and fit and pretty
With clear skin and polished pearl nails.
She obviously does no housework
Perhaps she has an au-pair
But what's that up there in the corner
A cob-web, I do declare!
Frances Fothergill

Our Street
It's got a bit o' character as our yon street,
Tho' it's none too clean and none too neat
But ther's them deawn't road and them next door
And them wit' babe as yells for evermooer.

Then ther's owd Sam as likes a pint a two
And woman oos 'usband beats 'er black 'n blue
Ther's loads 'a kids wi' 'oles in ther clooas
An 't' lad three dooers away, wit' drippin' nose.

Rent fella calls on a Freeday neet
But ther's nobody in or ther keep'in out' a seet
When't club man comes, it's a different matter
Weer all ont' street, 'avin a natter.

No, it's not much fun when thar's poor an' broke
Scratin' on 't' tip for a bit o' coke
But ther's gradely fowk 'as lives deawn our way
Ready to 'elp, neet or day.

We con 'ave a bit' a fun or shed some tears
Tell a few jokes, an 'ave a few beers
Cum in, sit deawn, pull up yon chair
We'll 'ave a bit 'o' crack, if thar's time to spare.
Glenda Boardman

Al Tuwallil Qatar
In this place sun or shade,
Nothing else.
Either the heat sears or it does not
And the white rock
Reflects its extremity.

Here it is light or dark,
Nothing gradual.
Now it is bright day, then it is night
And the deep desert
Sucks on infinity.

There stars punctuate black space.
Nothing obscures.
White floods of moon pierce the space
And the blushed heaven
Sings to eternity.
B S Burton

Lancashire North West
Of all the sights that I have seen
Of all the places I have been.
There's none that can compare
with Blackpool, Mecca of the North;
The grass is greener there.

There's golden sands and marching bands
and donkey rides for all.
And top-class entertainment
where one can have a ball.

To stroll along the Golden Mile
and view the famous Tower.
Or ride the great Big Dipper
with its exhilarating power.

When the weathers' mild
upon the Fylde
there's no place I'd rather be.
Every boy and girl
can have a twirl
in Blackpool by the sea.

You may visit Coney Island
or fly to sunny Spain.
But Blackpool illuminations
will tempt you back again.
John R Calvert

Rutland Water
Drowning Church,
Prayerless,
Cold.
Empty.
Winds romp and whisper
Through deserted aisles.
Disturbing no one.
Stirring only the stench of time.
The trees still nod and watch,
Their wet green light shading the water.
Where once congregations gathered together.
Frothy creations held firm
by white-gloved hands
on devout heads,
Announce the day is sanctified.
Today's Sabbath wind on Rutland Water
Stirs only the sails of the pleasure seekers.
The church peeps out from its watery bed,
Quietly observing another Genesis.
Elizabeth Kent

Our Great Britain
Think a little of our country
Stop, look around, and wait
At our ways, and old traditions
And why Britain is so great.

Scotland it has the thistle
tam-o'-shanter with a tilt,
They also have the sporran
And the pipers wear a kilt.

In Wales they have the daffodil
And a lovely great big leek
With music from the valleys
Or from a mountain peak.

There's Ireland with the shamrock
Known the whole world over
The only place you will find
A little four leaf clover.

The English have the bull dog
Looks so rugged and so rough
With a union jack across his chest
He is so strong and tough.

One lady we are proud to share
The most loved person ever seen
So wish her some peace and quiet
And God bless our lovely Queen.
Edward Dixon (Melly)

Preston 1950
Terraced red brick stand in line
Brass knockers, door knobs
Polished like medals,
Steps blancoed
Stiff at attention.

Barrack-like at the street end
Stands the mill.
Now it is shedding its weaving women
Deafened and shrill.

Soon
Clog marching
On stone cobbled setts
In lamplit rainshine
The men will come.

And in an hour, windows glowing
Pot steaming, pipe smoking,
And cinder warm
The terrace will stand easy.
William E Moore

Beach at Theologos
Love moved in silence upon us
Catching the dusky Aegean sky.
Our torch beam illuminating
The hidden curve of island life.
Identifying moths the size of sheep
Or seals their fat heads swinging
Indifferently away down the pebble beach
Past the basking fishing nets voracious
Fishermen resembling Willie Nelson or Christ.
While fish in small shoals hugged the drift.
Within our light we moved
Onto a jetty of rough stone
Fired at the Turkish coast
A scorched face blistering the dark.
And as the water curled between our toes
Toffee waves warmer than air
Pushed our bright heads close
Between two coastlines a shooting star
Pulsed and was bravely gone.
Love moved in silence upon us
That night on the beach at Theologos.
John A Stevenson

Brechin City

The Cathedral, the Castle so stately and tall.
That's Brechin City and we have it all.
The people are friendly and know everyone.
From Grannies to Grandads and everyone's son.

We have a grand river, the lovely Southesk.
Where the salmon are leaping and you hold your breath,
for another big leap reaching up for a fly,
at eventide as the sun sinks low in the sky.

October brings the tattie pickin', wee feets frozen,
een' a stickin', singing in the tattie larry,
slow doon driver whit's the hurry.

Off we go home at five o'clock, a bee-line for the stovie pot.
Washin' hands in soapy suds, peelin' onions, peelin' spuds.
The bairn's a' yellin' for their tea, another day and six pounds three.
Agnes Peal

Banff

B - the beauty of sunsoaked beach
A - animals changing shape
N - is the noise of the foghorned sea
F - the forming of fear, fret and foam
F - the frightening loud music
　　of shipwreck the rocks.
Allie Bartlett

My Town

What a dingy town it is,
My home town
All its glory gone and its
cotton spent
A canal where barges no
longer went,
It was my home town

Once a pit was its pride
Now inside a pub is where it's
laid off hide,
They've built a by-pass to miss it
And a superstore goes with it,
So you can't see Leigh
And that's my home town.
M A Aldridge

For the Bliss of Loneliness
'Tis for the bliss of loneliness
And nature's company;
For Heaven, thus a wilderness
Devoid humanity,
That oft' I roam the paths that wind
About the countryside,
Meandering in hope to find
Remoter parts to hide.

A place that has the magnitude
That I can wander free
Within its bounds of solitude,
Yet see no boundaries:
To roam amidst the peacefulness
Of nature - and Her voice;
At bliss with Her and loneliness,
And inwardly rejoice.
Harry Crompton Fils

To the Owl
The owl,
You magic bird of night,
So lovely in your flight.
Swift as an arrow to catch your prey,
You live by night and sleep by day.

High in your lofty perch,
Looking down on earth.
You miss not a thing,
Then suddenly you're on the wing,
Gliding, down, down, down.
You've seen a movement in the grass,
It's all over in a flash.
A cry, a squeal,
And you have your next meal.
Winnie Lee

My Cat Dances
In a scummy yard, by the old canal,
My cat dances.
He sees beauty in hideous things,
He takes his chances.

Love to him is the feeding time,
As certain as the day is long,
He has no memories of meadows green,
Bright blue days and birdsong.

I walk on air from the terminus,
My heart dances.
The world I knew left far behind,
I took my chances.

Could you doubt me now my love?
Could you doubt me at all?
With this sincerity oozing forth,
Could you doubt me at all?

The past is just a waste of time,
It could never haunt me.
When you say to me, 'Be good, be good,'
That's when you know I won't be.

I would not call you a waste of space,
I would not say that at all,
And when the rain falls,
Don't let your face
Be a vale of tears.
Andrew Callen

Autumn
Autumn days are with us once again.
The leaves, red and gold, falling like rain.
They are blown from the trees and carpet the ground.
When you walk through them, they make a rustling sound.
'Tis the sign of winter coming, cold winds and snow,
The leaves will have gone by then - nothing to show,
That once the trees had a mantle of green,
Where fruits and berries grew, and birds would be seen.
But autumn leaves must fall, just like the rain,
To make way for another spring, and life to begin again.
Just like the other seasons of the year,
Autumn has its beauty, red and gold, and a tear.
Ruby L Robinson

Lancashire
Lancs, is short for Lancashire,
Hills and vales, and dreaming spire,
Bustling towns, and waterways,
Shire horses, and brewery drays,
Cobbled streets, and homely pubs,
Foaming ale, and flower tubs,
Castle walls from by gone days,
Abbey cloisters, monks, and praise,
A county full of history

There's plenty here for all to see,
Its folks, hard workers, down to earth,
A love of life, of joy, and mirth,
Clog dancers, and walking days,
Tableaux decked in bright array,
Fish and chips, and Blackpool rock,
Easter bonnets, Sunday frock,
Garden parties, village fetês,
Black puddings, and chorley cakes,
Steam rollers, with engines bright,
Pendle Hill, witches flight,
Grouse moors, guns, and stately home,
Where even royalty can roam,
Always a welcome, here to be had,
From any true Lancashire lass or lad.
A Baker

My Pendle Hill
When you walk over Pendle
on a lovely spring day,
And see all the lambs
a prancing away,
And the cows in the meadow
All peaceful and still,
When you walk over Pendle,
O'er my Pendle Hill.

When you walk over Pendle
And the sun has gone down,
There are witches
on broomsticks flying around,
There are spells there for evil,
And spells there for right,
When you walk over Pendle
on any dark night.

When you walk over Pendle,
And the sun starts to rise,
And behold all the glory,
Or'e the land and the skies,
When you walk over Pendle,
With the sun in your hair,
When you walk over Pendle,
I will be there.
B Graham

Untitled
Lancashire, O' Lancashire,
County of great renown,
Of famous city and town,
Of Windermere and flats,
Where tourists trade with businessmen,
And are seen in fancy hats.
A county stretched from Cartmel,
Down to south-east Lancs,
From Barnaldswick to Southport,
From Pennine heights to
Blackpool's banks,
Was carved apart in '74,
With scarce a word of thanks,
A shire once known for humour,
Now part of seven countries ranks.
P Tipping

Chimneys
I'd look down from the coppice side
Where the brook, the fence, and pens collide,
Over the rec and through the wood,
And there like sentinels stood - the chimneys.

Each with a character of his own,
Of brick, timber, iron and stone,
Astride their mill, wheels, and forges,
Fire and steam in the air disgorges - like black demons.

And I knew they'd understood me grand,
For they'd puff and sigh and touch my hand,
With long shadows of the setting sun,
To dry the tears that would often come - such solace.

Then in the morgue of the wake week days
As we gambolled like lambs in the sand filled bays,
A hush would descend on the pointing fingers,
Like a shroud in suspension, touching and lingers - just resting.

But then coming home many miles away,
I would see them waving, as if to say,
It's crumpets for tea and Stanley's won,
The kettles on, come and see us Son - what a welcome.

Then there came a long vacation,
A scholarship ride to education,
Later on the world to see,
The chains were snapped, at last I was free - from the past?

I never returned until the day,
My grieving father passed away.
Compulsion took a farewell climb,
Among the sedge, the brook through time - to say hello.

But all there was to see and mourn
Was grass and stumps, and space forlorn,
For they'd been cruelly crushed and broken,
Whilst looms grew rusty, gone unspoken - why?

'Where were you?' the spirits cried,
To let them pillage, rape and ride
Back to Whitehall's' ivory towers,
Trampling Lancashire's finest flowers.

Amid my tears I made a vow,
To fight oppression and greed somehow,
And find a fairer truer vein,
From the blood of the slain - dear chimneys.
D Bertwistle

A Visit to Lancashire
If you've never been to Lancashire
You wont know what you've missed
Of the seaside towns, and countryside
and the gentle rolling mist.
The folks round here are friendly
They all nod or shake your hand
And pass the time of day with you
while on the streets they stand.

And eating out in Lancashire, is really quite a treat
especially in those country pubs
You'll find good grub to eat
While the rolling hills, and riversides
all beckon you to stay
and picnic on the hillsides
among the smell of new mown hay.

Now if you haven't been to Lancashire
Why don't you take that break
And come and see these friendly folk
Who offer tea and home-made cake.
You won't be disappointed, of that I truly say
For these gentle folk in Lancashire
Will truly make your stay.
Barbara C Boon

Nature's Picture
When walking in a country lane,
Sun shining bright, or in the rain,
Let your eyes behold, the wonders all around,
The sky above, the grassy ground.

Enveloping arms of every tree,
Nature reaches out to thee,
The birds that sing of cheerful note,
The *badger fox* and little *stoat*.

Wild flowers that dance, in the gentle breeze,
The leaves that fall with graceful ease,
Colours glowing all around,
A beautiful picture can be found.

The picture hangs not upon a wall,
This picture doesn't hang at all,
For nature's picture just lives free,
It's there for everyone to see.
Maud Eleanor Hobbs

Fox Hunt
A misty morning, damp and fresh,
A bugle sounds,
I must hide for my flesh
is the goal of this bloodthirsty
vicious game,
And now they are coming
with pleasure, not shame.

I run and I run and I run and I turn
my head, I can see them, I run
and I learn
no matter which way I run
they can tell
each place I've been
yes those dogs can smell.

Red men on horses they follow behind,
Black hats on their head don't hide what's on their mind.
With whips in their hands and spurs on their feet,
they'll chase and they'll chase until I'm dead meat.

Panting and choking I stop for a breath
but each stop I make brings me closer to death,
My heart, it is beating, so fast, it must burst
then over the hill, oh no, here come the first.
Barking and barking they're gaining on me
as I scramble through bushes and dodge past each tree.

I cannct keep running, how long can this last
before my short future turns into my past?
Instinct to live is my strength to keep running,
Dogs obey orders and so they keep coming,
Like man they enjoy it, yes them I amuse,
but the horses, they too, are just something to use.

I run and I try and I try and I cry,
Hot breath upon me, I know I must die.
My flesh will be torn, they'll spit out my fur,
My red coat made redder
than ever before,
My blood used to smear a beginner's head -
'Fox are vermin and better off dead!'
Jane McDowell

My Secret Garden
I have these lovely flowers,
All grown by fertile powers.
They seem to stir my emotions,
As if by spiritual potions.

The beautiful colours and shades,
Like lovely pictures which cascade.
I love to walk and touch,
To have my garden means very much.

It is a rare and simple thing,
The joy and pleasure that flowers bring.
Thank you Lord for this wondrous gift,
To give my heart a great big lift.
Liza Leece

School
The school bell rings out long and loud,
To hurry on, a motley crowd,
Polished boots and well scrubbed faces,
In the yard they take their places.
Woe betide, those not in line,
Punishment will fit the crime.
This was all so long ago.
Cheeky kids, of our today,
Fashion plates, with lots to say.
Mums, and dads arrange a rotor,
So the kids can go by motor.
Teacher says, 'Just call me John,'
Children don't know right from wrong.
Discipline has to come,
It must encourage everyone,
To look to the future, do their best,
Fate alone will do the rest.
J Chapman

The Mersey
How she winds from her hillside home,
Seeking the currents from the joint river foams,
Polluted by bye-gone satanic mills,
No longer the pure spring water from yon hills.

Ho! How she longs for the days,
When salmon and trout swam in her ways,
And her banks were the place to play,
Enjoying the full light of day.

Instead of buildings tall and forlorn,
Looking down on her with hatred and scorn,
Now the mill workers and mills all gone,
Can, now the river its battle be won.

To claim its right to be pure and clear,
And no civilisation to further fear.
To flow her true course out to the sea,
Her banks to be walked by workers now free,
From the drudge and the toil,
It's back the soil,
To eat food that's pure,
And not progress to fear,
To dreams of perfection,
That don't hold secretion, infection,
Rivers of toxins and waste,
Time! now to halt civilisation in haste.
John F Perkins

For Dornie
I watched the water's endless motion,
It echoed through my restless soul.
I viewed the current's ceaseless rolling,
In ethereal silence of tranquil toll.

And in my silence I longed to stay,
In my solitude cast by encumbering days.
Apart from the world which adopted my time,
Apart from the world, corrupted by binds.

Here there is beauty, sublime as fortold.
Here there is truth and awe to behold.
Here is what's real, yet strangely divine,
An eternal experience, suppressed by time.
Guyan John Porter

Deep in the Heart of Govan
Culture is deep
In the heart of Govan,
Standing regal
Blonde and tall,
The pearce
The institute for people.
It holds within
Its many halls,
Plays to tantalise
And tease,
Situation comedy
Variety for everyone
The serious, the funny.

There is a class
For keeping fit,
There's a club for judo,
Here's where humble
folk can meet,
To have the choice
To raise a voice.

Culture is near
Culture is here
Culture is deep
In the heart of Govan.
Ruby A Graham

Tartans' Rising
I stood and watched the Tartans' rising
In my Scottish sky,
Blood red plumes now streaked with golden
Were its battle cry.

I stood and listened to its silence
Ghostly in its peace,
The fiery glow now a whisper
Dappling through the trees.

I stood and watched the salmon leaping,
Saw the crystal fall,
Heard the laughter of the river
As it sang its call.

I stood and watched strong backs abending
Working on the earth,
Rich fertile loam now awaiting
The blessings of rebirth.

I stood and watched the trawlers sailing,
Wished them safe return,
I saw the purple of the heather
Nestling by the burn.

I stood and listened to the pipes,
Clear sweet melody,
And I remembered what this land
So dearly means to me.
Glen Summers

Loch Leven
There lay the Loch in perfect splendour,
Encircled by its belt of trees;
The lapping waves their song do render,
While ruffled by the gentle breeze.

On every side the hills stand out,
In beautiful and bright relief;
Which once have echoed to the shout,
Of some fierce ancient Highland Chief.

Out from the shore there can be seen
An island with a ruined castle;
Which once had housed a captive queen,
And been the home of lord and vassal.

I love you so, my dear Loch Leven!
For beauty nothing thou dost lack;
To leave you now my heart is grieving,
Until the time that I get back.

Although I journey far from home,
And sorrow o'er the friends I'm leaving
Ever shall my fond thoughts roam,
And bring me back to thee, Loch Leven.
Alexander K Sampson

The Restless World
The nights have gone now or so it seems
And stars lost in endless headlight beam,
There is no sleep only eternal day,
In a hastening world
Where *time* is at a premium for speed.

There is no rest, no quiet street,
No door left idling on the latch,
No family complete beneath the eaves
Settled together in peaceful dreams.

There is no stillness or desire to stay
Free from movement and perpetual chase;
Like angry bees from a disturbed hive
They frantically strive for confusion's lead.

All are blind and unresponsive
To the calm of seasonal pace,
Tormented, lost, in a futile race
Where fatigue and destruction
Go hand in hand,
And nature despairs at the stupidity
                              of man.
Edna Dixon

Reflections of Promise
Above the crag
Still softly lit by the western sky,
Stands the moon.
Bathed in the full light of the sun.

Here among the naked trees
We await the frosted winter's night
And as our darkness grows,
So too does the brightness
Held steady in that pitted crescent face.

Soon the colours will fade,
Familiar things lapse into obscurity
And our only light, reflected.
Borrowed and bounced off one
Who having no light in himself
Becomes to us a lamp,
A guide and a hope.

As we turn our eyes
Away through the laced tracery
Of the trees, beyond the now blackened crag,
Upwards, we see the sun,
Bright and strong and pure.

For now we borrow the eyes of the moon,
But when the earth has turned,
Twisting the mooon into its heavy rim
We too shall see.
On us directly shall those immediate rays descend.
Hope fulfilled shall pass,
Enveloped in the splendour of day.
Simon Bull

The Silvery Tay
The River Tay runs fast and deep
For many miles, no time for sleep
As it forges to its journey's end
Both as a foe and as a friend.

What wondrous force sustains this flow
At dead of night and in morning's glow
The frisky waters are seen to play
As they surge along without delay.

A turbulent torrent or peaceful trickle
How can such beauty be so fickle
Meandering down thru' pastures green
Then raging o'er a rocky scene.

It passes Aberfeldy's town
Glistening like a jewelled crown
As it flows beneath the bridge of Wade
Towards Dunkeld like some huge lade.

It serves the ancient Royal city
Of bustling Perth, but oh!- the pity
When the elements make the river swell
And causes havoc to those who dwell.

An Emperor from ancient Rome
Surveyed the dancing, glitt'ring foam
Of turgid waters flowing by
Behold the Tiber was his cry.

The Carse of Gowrie's fertile plain
From the River Tay made its gain
Like Bonnie Dundee, for many a day
Has thriven by the Silvery Tay.
J Emslie Lamond

My Hame Toon
Montrose it is a bonnie toon,
Here aside the sea.
Its golf course, beach and links o' green
Mean a' the world tae me.
We locals hae a funny name
We're ca'ed the *Gable-enders,*
An' ye kin ponder whit that means
As ye wander roond the *danders*,
We have a fine lang high street,
Wi shops o' ilka kind,
An you'll find the fowk real freendly
If to stop them you've a mind.
We've a centre fur sports an' a swimming pool.
Bit mair pubs than kirks is the general rule.
The Glaxo is the place fur jobs
Though there's plenty on the dole.
Bit fowk here ull gie ye a helpin' hand
So's the worst times ye kin thole.
It's nae far fae here tae Dundee or Aibirdeen,
Ye kin ging wi' bus or train
Bit farivir ye gang ye kin be assured
Ye'il be glaid tae be hame again.
Aye there's strife an' wars a' roond the world
Bit it's here ah like tae bide
'Cause ah find peace an harmony
Richt here in auld Tayside.
Joan Christie

Ormiston

'Let's praise Ormiston and its charms,
the Auld Tyne Brig and the Hopetoun Arms,
the Hoosin' Scheme abune the Dam,
wi' bright Prefabs no one can sham.
The Public Park now looking trig,
a braw New Schule o'erlooks the Brig.
The Dam that once ran tae the Mill,
its traces can be seen there still.
The wide Main Street well lined wi' trees
that in the summer scent the breeze.
There's no the like in any village,
when those trees are decked wi' foliage
and wise was he that drew the plan,
he must have been a superman
to plant the trees in their right places
and decorate those open spaces.
Then build the Cross into the scheme,
a happy thought, a kindly theme.
and make a Green for folks to dance,
which in those days was their only chance.
Then Moffat's statue at the end,
is sure to interest your friend
when coming here on short vacation,
and taking a walk doon by the Station.
The braw new Kirk that decks the Glebe,
wi' the Manse behind supplying the need
of a worthy Cleric who gained honours
and brought respect upon the Donors.
The Institute a long felt want,
where Pensioners meet, their views to chant.
Behind the Memorial of greater fame,
from which the Institute takes its name
in respect of Heroes in their prime
who went forth to toe the line
and brought victory to these shores
amidst the plaudits and the roars
of a semi drunken Nation,

which seemed to me bore no relation
to a just and lasting Peace
of which the World needs a lease.
But to my muse of all the charms,
I'm bound to add those of the Farms.
Likewise the gardens rich with fruit
set off the landscape without a doot.
Thomas Davidson

Dingwall Slumbers
Claws clinging to MacDonald's grey stone tower
Way up on Mitchell Hill
A black rook stares fixedly below
But Dingwall slumbers still.

With glinting eye and beak apart
He studies autumn's hue
Rests in some ancient Poplar trees
With grave stones for his view.

Black polished wings stirring in the wind
With dry leaves falling fast
See the silent canon, gathering close
Beneath October's bitter blast.

Screaming loud the swirling bats
Haunt the vacant tower
The rook blinks his knowing eye,
And silently greets his funeral hour.

Dingwall town still smug, continues unaware
While the black bird awaits impending doom
He tries stretching his ragged wings to leave
But is trapped, hooded 'neath the gloom.

Now lying stiff and deathly still
The earthworms have their feast
Swiftly winter came with icy rage
A cemetery, no place for man or beast.
Rosaline H MacDonald

A Walk Down Scotsburn Glen
To the heights of Cnoc Un Duin,
From the ruins of Coulpleasant Farm,
Let's hope and pray for the sun,
In deep winter's frozen charm.

So on past brooding Lochan Dubh,
Covered now by sky of blue,
And on further to Easterglen,
Once filled with braver men.

Look up now to Barnschlay Hill,
And down to St George's well,
Let's rest now and have our fill,
Not for us the open fell.

Heading off to Westerglen,
Sadly past more ruins of men,
Soon be now our journey's end,
Shed a tear lonely Scotsburn Glen.

(Scotsburn Glen: A small glen in Easterross not far from Tain Dotted with various ruins, Coulpleasant, Easterglen, Westerglen and others.)
Brian Kershaw

My Village Home
Have you ever been to Angus and seen our bonny glens?
Or travelled oot fae Dundee, ower Lumley Den,
Oh! What a panoramic view, there before your eyes,
As on the far horizon, the Grampians kiss the sky.

The hills are blue wi' heather, the trees and grass sae green,
It brings a lump intae my throat, to view this lovely scene.
For nestling in the hollow is my birthplace and my home,
There's nae place else on earth sae dear, nae matter where I roam.

Oft hae I wandered by the burn, that flows down to the Dean,
Or climbed the brae to Hunter's Hill, where Romans once had been.
Majestic in the hollow stands Glamis Castle, steeped in lore,
And stretching out from East to West, the Valley of Strathmore.

Our village boasts a *Folk Museum*, a fine kirk and a manse,
A schule, a smiddy, and a bank, and a hall where we can dance,
Then if you want a first class meal, visit *Strathmore Arms*
You'll get a warm welcome, frae the freendly folk o' Glamis.

We also have three village shops, that attend to all our wants,
A drapers-cum-Post office, for either socks or stamps,
A bakers shop-cum-grocer and a hardware shop that sells,
Newspapers, books and candy and garden seeds as well.

With all these things to offer, can you really wonder why?
I love my little *village home*, where money cannot buy,
The things that matter most in life, contentment, loving friends,
Nature's beauty all around and God's love to all extends.
Dorothy Keith

Discord

On forest paths made strangely red
By needles dropped from long-grown larch,
There's respite from the troubled world
Beneath the sheltering woodland arch.

Deer merge with bracken, squirrels with light,
A half hid wren reproaches me.
From Nature's stronghold comes the strength
To combat harsh adversity.

A roar - a scream - a lingering growl -
Two giant arrows cleave the air.
Symbols of strife, they charge my mind
With images of sad despair.
Joy Carruthers

Riches
Today I saw a rainbow
and wondered if it's true
that at the end if you should dig
there's a pot of gold for you.
Then I stood there thinking
my what a wonderful sight
now I know what you mean
the treasure is within your light.
Steven Dawson

Lament for Lost Trees
Listen to this tearful lamentation,
'Gainst felling fine trees a protestation.
On a slope, 'neath a spacious sky,
Outlined in splendour three sycamores soared high.
From spreading branches bird song gave delight,
While call of hidden owls would fill the night.

There the black rooks, all clamouring loudly,
Boasted of family squabbles proudly.
And squawking seagulls - wheeling and crying,
For haven from storm tossed seas came flying,
Light breezes stirred and set the trees dancing.
While sunlight across the leaves came glancing.

An enchanting scene, it brought me rapture
With brush, muse inspired, tree portraits I'd capture.
None more precious, none lovelier than these,
In line once stood our sentinel trees.
Our landscape is ruined, our hearts are sore,
A treasure is lost, we can never restore.

Sawn logs into heaps are callously tossed
No living trees left to sparkle in frost.
No branches laden in winter's snow fall,
Nor leaf buds to break at springs urgent call.
Sadly, the wood owl has nowhere to perch,
Further afield disturbed song birds must search.

The moon stares down coldly from empty skies.
No playing now behind branches, she sighs,
The sky glowers o'er a desolate hill,
No more with joy will our saddened hearts fill,
In landowner's power, nature is held,
Irretrievable, our fine trees are felled.
M Sharpe

Aberdeen
Our marischall college shining bright
in sunshine or floodlit at night.
Our long majestic Union Street
a thoroughfare, it's hard to beat
but what in springtime mostly thrills?
We see a million daffodils.

Down to the harbour tourists flock
to view the shipping in the dock
or perhaps visit a park or two
believe me we have quite a few
but what delights the eyes and noses?

To see and smell a million roses.
I know throughout this Isle of ours
there's other buildings, parks and flowers
and when I can love to go
to view the sights they have to show
nevertheless I'm always keen
to come back home to Aberdeen.

Whether you come to work or play
we make sure you enjoy your stay
we welcome you with open arms
to share with us the city's charms
we welcome you by deed and word
true to our motto *Bon Accord.*
George Cooney

Renfrewshire
Haunt of Kings and great liner Queens,
O'er which Ben Lomond keeps watch . . . or so it seems!
Towns and villages where men aspire
To that heartland which is Renfrewshire!

From Johnstone famed for engineering,
Bridge of Weir's tanned leather is quite endearing.
Home is Kilbarchan if born a *Habbie*
But the jewel in the crown is Paisley Abbey!

Once landed gentry had their vast estates
Now developers do business at their gates.
Cunningham, Fleming, Semple, Coats,
Their legacy still their name promotes!

Steeped in history its Cathedral sits,
Having proudly endured the war time blitz!
As Paisley Pattern the thread mills spun
For Paisley buddies and everyone!

Like a spouse supporting its work and play
The River Clyde makes Greenock's shipyards pay.
With Glasgow Airport quite near its sands,
The connecting door to foreign lands!

Well known to Bruce and home to Wallace,
A scenic cradle when seeking solace!
With Tannahill 'mongst its sons and daughters,
Inspiring verse in school wean's jotters!

Enshrined in the patchwork we call Strathclyde,
It's Renfrewshire that is the pride!
No accolade could be much higher
Than to be hailed as one from Renfrewshire!
Eileen Mulholland

Garden in Bloom
The scent of the roses rise up in the air
After the rainfall it starts to fair
The cool wet ground is like glistening dewdrops
The pitter patter of the rain from the leaves soon stops.

The rows of aster stand to attention
Also the petunias, not to mention
The foxgloves in all their glory stand
The carnations think they're the pick of the land.

To the left of the garden grows the large willow tree
And climbing up the wall is the perfumed sweet pea.
Lifelike pot gnomes are scattered here and there,
And cheeky little daisies are growing everywhere.

'Round the trellised archway creeps dark green ivy
Overseeing the pansies who are looking so lively
A profusion of lilies lurk in the shadows
And African violets stand in their rows.

Situated in a corner is a rhododendron bush
Peeping through the leaves is a sweet singing thrush.
A lovely mass of colour all around I see
The flowers soon attract a small bumble bee.

The hothouse is full of red ripe tomatoes,
A gardener is whistling as he finishes his chores.
Carrots, turnips and onions are all in a batch
Making up the numbers in the vegetable patch.

A country garden should never be without
Loads of veg both lean and stout
Still to me the flowers are best
And a garden in bloom is where to find rest.
Vera Skelton

Summer's Day
Sunlight at morning,
Beautiful, promising:
Windows wide open
To warmth everywhere.

Sunlight at midday,
Strident and clamouring
Breaking through shutters;
Heat, dryness and dust.

Sunlight at evening,
Long shadows falling,
Foretelling moonlight,
Coolness and peace.
Irene Attwell

The Picture Window
As I gaze out to the hills beyond,
It fills my heart with a joyous song.
Over the grass and across the sea,
The distant hills beckon to me.
The beautiful trees, the birds on their wings,
The peace and quietness
Happiness brings.
This part of England is the
Perfect place,
To sit and enjoy from life's mad race.
There is the ever changing scene
Much nicer than a TV screen.
The tide comes in on a bore
and laps the grass near the shore.
The sky is blue, clouds white
And grey come speeding along the way.
We get the grey and mauve lights
And gold for all to see,
But the sun set is the most
wonderful sight for me.
D Highman

Mannanin's Sky
Touched by colour
The autumn sky
Whispered daylight
A soft goodbye.
Layers of pink
In soft repose
Stabbed by streaks
Of amber gold.
My pagan heart
Is moved to prayer
When Glory fills
The very air.
Amanda Comish

This Place is Mine
The dark hills roll from a sky of pale blue,
Cascading in green to the beachy land;
Where rough waves, crashing, are stealing the sand.
At morning, it was here where the guillemots flew.

When grey mists gather in the hazy air
They swell to a dark and distant rain,
Soon to drip from clouds which clip Traprain
Turning the blues black. But the winds will fair

This bay, and the clouds will clear to the sun;
The golden light will dance on the sea,
Like diamond angels longing to be free,
And cast long shadows for the night to come.

And as the burning light gently drops low,
The hills and sea are splashed soft reds and pinks,
The white Bass darkens as the sun slowly sinks
And a glittering array of stars then glow

Above; where now the angels are at rest.
The waves dreamily lapping, occasionally slap
The sand as the warm breeze tugs and tired wings flap
Under the gentle moon beams which kiss each crest.

The moon sails across the night's sky in time
And all the stars fall to the salty sea,
Where mystery lives and dangers there be.
Lights grow colours change. This place is mine.
Christopher Newman

Ode to Craigievar Castle by a National Trust Guide
Near Alford, in the Howe O' Mar, an Aberdeenshire gem
Lies the noble rock o'r Craigievar, castle o' Forbes fame.
Throu aa the years I looed it weel, I kent its story fine
Tae tell tae aa fae far an wide, an ambition wis o' mine.

O' Craigievar, I bless the day I spok tae Dave an asked
If I could tak the tourists roon a spik abbot yer past.
Wide granite steps lead tae the Hall, I gie them aa the spiel
O' Danzig Willie an his wife - I learnt it at the squeel.

Across the wye's the withdrawin room, far ladies o' lang syne
Wid sit an hae a news 'afore they'd tak' a gless o' wine,
The Tartan Room is up the stair wi' portraits aa 'aroon
O' Danzig Willie, Reed Sir John, an Bishop Patrick's loon.

Up mair steps an' throu the place far hoosekeepers wid bide
Intae the Queens room far the bed fair takes the place o pride.
Anither race o stairs an syne the castle widens oot
Tae corbellin an towers aroon, an mony a fancy spoot.

The blue room his an eerie fin o' spirits nae at peace
Did Reed Sir John regret the deed that made the Gordon cease?
The Nursery is a fair sized room wi sleepin quarters next
Far little forbeses did their sums an likewise learnt their text.

Abeen them aa the Lang Room lies - it faces North an Sooth,
Wi' tales o' washin hingin there, passed on bi word o' mooth,
Next door the servant quines wid sleep, box beds held three or four,
Syne doon the secret stair we gang back tae the first floor.

An doon the steps tae dungeon dark far peer souls wid have pined
Fin ladies up abeen their heed hid been baith wined an dined,
Oot throu the studded door an yett tae hae an ootside view
Remindin aa o' fairy tales - Craigievar! A toast tae you!
Lorna Alexander

Cathedral
A big Cathedral very old
can tell some tales
that no one's told.

At night they walk around the hall
the dead, the living
I wonder if they have been told.

About the past, of days gone by
when all the Kings of England
used to come and pray.
Lilian Coombs

Dumfriesshire
Dumfriesshire you hold me in your womb,
Even if there is no room,
You will be my tomb,
Fairies and goblins inhabit you,
Spirits and mystical hues,
And I will die with you and pay my dues.

Dumfriesshire a velvet ray,
Encloses my soul as I look to the sun
As you begin the day
And smell your sweetness
Enclosing your smile
Folding gold eternal.
Jane S Simpson

East Kilbride
Where you go 'round to the school
And 'round to the store,
Then 'round to your friends
And roundabout more.
There's an ice rink, swimming pool,
Sport centres too.
Calderglen, with the nature walk
Plus the children's zoo.

Golf courses, bowling alley, discos,
Lots of pubs.
A nine screen cinema,
And a dozen different clubs,
There's lot of shops which are
All under one roof.
It's great living here,
You want more proof . . .

Well, go to the theatre,
A panto or a play.
And new businesses opening up,
Every other day.
A visit to bingo where
You might have a win
Or take a trip to Denmark
And visit our twin.
But maybe just go down the road
To the banks of the Clyde.
Though I'm sure you'll soon be running back
To bonnie East Kilbride.
Jacqueline Gill

Stevenston
S tevenston is where I live
T he best wee town people give, give, give,
E ven when you walk around
V ery good people can be found.
E ntertainment everywhere
N otice how the people care, care, care,
S tevenston is where I live
T he best wee town people give, give, give,
O pen hearts and people who care
N o other town could ever compare.
Rayma Barclay

East Lothian
East Lothian, opened their hearts doors,
To welcome, the people of Bosnia!
And they came to live here!
Instead of living in fear!
With a breath of fresh God's air!
Now they can live, without a care!
From the love, from the people, which they share!
From one disabled ex-serviceman!
Who knows what it's like to be loved!
J McWithers

Banished Waters
The swaying rushes whisper at the old mere's rim,
Their ceaseless murmur rising at the wind's capricious whim.
They dream of an empire, where the broad waters stood,
And they, the green-robed courtiers, rose proud above the flood.

Unhindered, still they flourished, down time's uncounted years,
Guarding well their kingdom in ranks of close-packed spears.
In solitude they multiplied, nor rival ever knew,
But dreamed away the centuries time granted as their due.

No need to fear intrusion, who rule by right divine;
Their dynasty was absolute, where the watered acres shine.
But territorial conquest, the ancient curse of man,
With scourge of desecration, reverses nature's plan.

Man came, he saw, he coveted the tracts of hidden land;
He sought to force the proud mere's will to bow to his command.
And so, against the natural law, man set his stubborn face,
And drained away the lifeblood from off that quiet place.

The courtiers' green robes faded - their host's support removed:
Both sun and man destroyed their roots, once shielded by the flood.
And now a rich and fertile plan, where no man's foot yet trod,
Must bear the plough upon its back, to turn the virgin sod.

Usurping man has tilled and sown for many years gone by,
And where the banished mere once stood, great seas of gold
                                                    now lie.
But see, with arrogance and courage, amidst the tall sprung grain,
The rushes rise defiant, and fringe the mere again.
M M Williams

November
November rain,
  high fell tops invisible
  merging with the leaden sky
paths awash, usurped by infant streams
  of this wet autumn's heavy rains
the ghyll's swollen waters
  dashing, swirling, foaming;
  their hypnotic roar enveloping,
  isolating us from all other sound
the tarn serene, ghostly, a brimming bowl
  accepting without protest
  the endless rain
dying bracken, leaves deepest russet, purple,
  limp and sad;
  defiant amber stalks with unexpected strength
  trapping our unwary feet
a single, fallen, rowan berry,
  vibrant, crimson, on the dun-brown path
gentle faced sheep, curious,
  white heads turning as we pass
  in the softening light
fairy tale cottages hugging the fell side,
  their lighted windows sending warmth
  along the darkening dale
tiny bats speeding crazily, skilfully,
  over our heads in the growing dusk.
Margaret R Williams

My Imaginary Animal
My imaginary animal
is full of different things.
It's got three heads and fourteen tails
and lots of golden wings.

One head is blue, the middle green,
the third one it is pink.
It's got five eyes on every head,
but still it cannot wink.

Body so sleek with layers of scales,
which shine and glow at night.
Feet of a bird and claws so sharp,
that give people a terrible fright.

I'm glad that my animal, is just in my head
I don't have to feed him at all.
But it looks after me when I go to sleep.
Just a picture high up on my wall.
Helené Duerden (10)

Keeping Time
This brown ribbon road
pitted with space and stone
reaches its ditch across the dry moor.
Where water rolls, sending the drum of its music
down the wet crevasses, to the earth's clay core.
And its rhythm feeds the thunder
of the spit and break of sole on hard track
unleashed, as it spurts its plume
into dry air, fastened
until its fingers spread outwards
through bolts of once belled heather
to spatter in the roots of peaty pools
to ripple out at the track's dark edge.

Here the thirsty traveller drinks
watching the shining city cling
to the veins of the valley floor.
And there is light still
in small windows of the sky
pinpricks, bursting here and here
upon its frame, as rose tucks into grey
above the cloak of the hooded hills.
And the traveller weighs his journey
with each foot's fall
with the shadow painted by each passing step
with the burden lifted to each bent shoulder
with each breath of the slow sky
as silence rolls down its steady shutters
on the curve of the watching land.
Pat MacKenzie

The County of Fife
In '74, new state legislation,
Made Fife unique unto our nation.
The kingdoms name remained intact,
Because Fifers couldn't face the fact
Tho' a thousand years had gone before
We couldn't use our name no more.

Once here we had coal and Limestone quarries
But since they filled so many lorries,
There's nothing left around these parts
Except for youths with broken hearts
They cannot find a job; no chance
And employers lead them quite a dance.

To make it worse the elders blame them
For crimes and troubles, and they name them
Don't forget, we created this situation,
These youths have never run the nation.
Maybe elders grudge the youths their leisure,
They worked fifty years, to earn that pleasure.

This county as named, has rightly been famed,
For men of perspective and brain,
In this kingdom of treasure, as tho' made to measure
Where King James said of old,
Fifes, fringes of gold,
Are my pleasure to behold.

There's no County can boast such a bounty you'll see
Where our Seniors can travel by bus and rail free.
By looking after our own,
And the kindness shown,
Then were bound to be known,
As that place, we are pleased to call home.
Ian MacFarlane

Border River
(This poem is dedicated to my late husband William R Murray for his love of the river Tweed.)

Feel a pride deep down inside
That Peebles is my home
Though the world is wide I must confide,
I never want to roam.
Give me the hills of my native town,
The Tweed as it flows by
Rolling along like a happy song.
Its beauty will never die.
Border river there you go
On your restless way
Many miles you have to flow
Until you reach the sea.
Through days and nights
When silver salmon leapt the caulds
Moonlight on scales a glimmer

O'er rugged land, across the rocks
Down the valleys, glen, wild, lonely spots,
Sometimes you're dirty Tweed
Sometimes you're silvery Tweed.
Sometimes you're restless Tweed.
On your way to the sea.
Janet Murray

The Waiting Room
The clock ticks healthily on,
The hour chimes, one, two, three,
Nearly time for tea.
'Shall we watch television dears?'
Such a bright cheerful voice.
Is this all I am kept alive for?
To listen to the chimes of a clock?
To be asked, no told to watch TV
My life is over now, I have had my fun.
I'm not deaf nor dumb
Though no-one asks what I would like.
A prisoner in this worn out shell
Aged and wrinkled, my brain tired.
I want to sleep,
To go quietly to my peace
I am entitled to that much surely,
No more the ticking clock
Feeling the long dragging hours,
Not realising day or night
Week or month.
I'm tired, let me sleep,
Let me pass on to my long earned rest
Don't pity my infirmity,
Don't prolong my disability,
Let me go on to God's eternity,
Let me sleep, the last long sleep.
Linda M T Edwards

Love
As darkness falls and I look to the sky
And see the beauty of this world,
And wonder why it isn't known to those,
So engrossed in this and that, and what they own,
Beneath their feet, if they look around
Lots of beauty can be found.
All God's creatures however small
Have importance like us all
The grass so green, the sky so blue
Glittering like diamonds, the morning dew,
If your ears hear - listen
If your eyes see - see
From light to dark,
Miracles and beauty there will be.
A single rose, a friendly face, some how we feel
God's grace, and know,
That he is here to show, the beauty, of maybe,
Just love.
Love is a fragile thing, a miracle to find
And if you have this precious gift, must nurture,
In a kind, of way, that makes your miracle last,
Forever and a day.
A new born babe, a precious birth, and the moments
That were filled with mirth.
A gentle smile, the softest touch, a tender look,
It doesn't take much, so look around - lots of
Beauty can be found.
B Lancashire Frain

Snowflakes
Snow flakes are falling
They make not a sound,
And the earth slumbers on
As they cover the ground.

Dancing and swirling
They touch and caress,
The tip of my nose
Then the hem of my dress.

Holly boughs glisten
With berries bright red,
And crisp is the path
I have chosen to tread.

Snow drops in splendour
Around me abound,
And the earth gently sighs
As they cover the ground.
Margaret Joy

The Eagle's Cry
The moon sleeps and the sun is obscured by clouds,
Somewhere below, a lake lies, hidden by a deep white fog,
Up here, in the mountains, the air is cold,
A fresh breeze blows through the towering peaks,
And from on high, a piercing Eagle's cry,
As she scans the lands below for food, to feed her young,
All she sees is a land locked in the cold grip of winter,
Where everything is white and nothing moves,
Up here, icy fingers crack the cold bare rocks,
Forcing fragments to slide to the scree mass below.
Up here, all is silent and all is still,
Breathing the air, my throat tastes the chill,
I huddle against cold naked rock, half frozen to death,
Waiting for her to return again,
As she circles 'round and 'round, still searching for food,
On a thermal that leads ever higher,
Towards the heavens and the sun,
Who's warmth I need, but who's face is hidden from me,

By dawn clouds that hang so low,
And below me, I can barely see the lake,
The place where I camped, just a few hours before,
And who's silent waters revived and awakened me,
Then filled me with purpose, as I began this trek,
So now, here I am surrounded by regal peaks,
Sitting on my throne, in this castle in the sky,
Waiting for the sun's rays to touch my face,
And its warmth to enlighten me . . .
Matthew Henderson

Life
The world is ours for us to see
The stars above, the budding tree
Each new day in us should wake
A fuller life for us to take
There's plenty of room for you and me
If only we will look and see!
The birds that sing up high above
Telling us about new love
New life beginning to take shape
A miracle that only God can create
Let us an example be
To all we know and accompany
We will have no time to feel depressed
If we use what's given
Share all the rest
Happy indeed we'll be
Margaret Walker

The Great Rift Valley
It is here that it all began - the Origin of Man!
In Equatorial Africa, the Cradle of the Universe lies.
From Nyanza, Turkana, Baringo, Naivasha through Masai
To Kilimanjaro's snows - who knows, but can in fact surmise.

Alert now, as knotted groups of starving souls meet and cry
With aching hunger, beside receding once emerald inland seas,
Immensely stocked with fish and a canopy of humid rainy sky.
Honking geese and flamingo, and the fish eagle's call on breeze,
Evoke the wild in the annals of the Soul, and aura of Eternity.
Running naked here, dusty stick-like charcoal homeless kids,
Pot-bellied disproportionately, waifs, bonded in fraternity, and in pity.
At once a dignified emaciated Elder compassionately forbids
Their desperate begging - in modulated tones he doth communicate,
In Kiswahili thus; Wazungu wetu, they all crave toys and clothes,
Little shoes and hats, and such things you discard at your gate
                                        for dustmen.
We too are Christians. Do you ever suppose our simple need will
ever be met, or don't you Westerners practice the creed.
Tom Powell

Observation Tower
From the treelike tower, from the tower like a tree,
We watched the birds and the birds watched we.
As they're saluting marsh the curlews creek,
For getting no oil their gates rust-squeek.

Shellfish, shoal-fish, shadows on shale,
Under woods and the weeds and splintering rail
Of would-fish waders winging to dine,
Shallow-fish, shy-fish, sheltering shine.

Birds fish. Shoal fish lurk in murked brine.
Shallows slap, lapping the tune of time,
Sun rings gold waves, bobbed boat slapsings.
Clouds breeze over. Lapwings flap wings.

Soft wind blowing, rustling rush,
Tripping the ripples of dimpled marsh.
Purple mud where curlews curl,
As we watch from our hides their feathered whirl.
Jenni Meredith

Rules
When you first start school
You're told to follow the rules
Don't do this, and don't do that
Or you will probable get a slap,
Don't let you nails grow long
Or they will say that is wrong
They tell you what clothes to wear
And how to wear your hair.
When the bells go you walk out in file
If you run you'll be kept in for quite a while
And when you leave school it's just the same
There are rules to follow over and over again,
You can't do nothing without filling in a form
From the day you are born
To the day you are dead and gone
There will always be someone waiting with a form.
Eileen Kyte

Somerset
From the Mendips to the Quantocks,
From the Quantocks to the sea,
Let us roam the hills and valleys leisurely
We will start at Dunster Village, with its quaint old cobbled streets
Graced by its famous Castle, set in grounds so exquisite.

Wandering thro' the country lanes we find primroses galore
Stopping to gaze through gateways at undulating Exmoor.
The cows slowly move, and sheep softly graze,
As we sigh at the breeze, that comes floating o'er the plain.

Then off again through countryside, so lush and so green,
And every mile or so are churches, and more churches to be seen.
We stop at Weston Zoyland, 'tis a famous one they say
Where the troopers put their dying, after Battle affray
We ponder as we gaze at the roof so high,
Admiring the carvings of beauty so fine.

Now we climb to Cheddar, admiring all the while
For the sunshine and shadow, dapple hills, for many a mile
The Gorge, with its awe inspiring cliffs, in every hue and shade
Are mighty grim reminders of a Prehistoric age.

Now we are on the plain once more,
And we make our way to Wells,
Treading the way the monks once trod,
The cathedral rings its bells;
Listening to the clamour, as their messages they toll,
They speak proud tales of Somerset,
We stand silent, one and all.
Dorothy Blackwell

Wanderer's Dream
Home town how I love you,
I miss you each day more.
Your cliffs tall grey, and rugged,
That stretch along your shore.
Rough narrow roads, pathways,
That wind uphill, then down
To meet the tidal river,
Which beautifies you, my home town.

Your castles speak of history,
When Cornishmen were bold,
And fought the fore unaided,
Or so the stories told,
Of wrecking barques, and smuggling,
Those skirmishes at night
Speak not of cowardly weakness,
But hearts of steel and might.

And now the scene is peaceful,
The little boats lie moored,
In summer to the quayside,
In winter they are stored,
The ships that pass bring cargoes,
Of friendship and goodwill,
They anchor safely in the port,
Beneath the rising hill.

And when my wandering's over,
To port I'll swiftly sail,
And cast my anchor in that land
Of sunshine rain and hail,
To settle in contentment
On Cornwall's welcome shore,
Thanking old Mother Earth
For this good portion from her store.
Morwenna Bateson

Cottage Life
Living in the countryside
Is where I want to be
In a cottage I reside
It is home to me.

Snug and warm in the winter
Cosy by the fire
Chopping logs, getting a splinter
But I never tire.

Chimneys covered in thick black soot
Ashes in the grate
Dropping logs upon my foot
That's the bit I hate.

Spiders lurk in every nook
Cobwebs drape the beams
Dust blankets every book
That's cottage life it seems.

The wind comes through the window panes
The snow melts through the roof
Puddles appear when it rains
But living here is proof.

That wind and rain can beat my home
And though my home is tatty
From it I will never roam
Although I must be scatty.
Tresca Tucker

Countryside Desecration
O' to be free, like a bird in the clouds
Far from the hustle and bustle of crowds
Away from roads thronged with lorries and cars
And gaze at the wondrous beauty of stars.

One could look below, on the frailty of man.
And the havoc created in life's short span
See the destruction to seas, rivers and land
Then they will say, it's all carefully planned.

Vast acres of forest and land torn asunder
In their quest for coal, they ravage and plunder
No fields of wild flowers, no woodland for bird.
Only time raucous noise, or machines can be heard.

Dry stone walls down the years have withstood winter's blast
Are now disappearing, a thing of the past
Rows of posts and wire, are now in their place
In the eyes of the behold, no beauty, no grace.

Effluent from land fouls river and stream
No longer the waters, sparkle and gleam,
Where once darting minnows and tadpoles would flay
It now dank smelling, muddy and grey.
David L Rae

The Sea
A spinster lives on the same floor as me
And says that she misses the sound of the sea.
She never noticed when the sea was there,
But now that it's gone,
She wishes she'd cared.
Leo Roberts